BRING YOUR "A" GAME

The 10 Career Secrets of
The High Achiever

Robert J. McGovern

SOURCEBOOKS, INC.®
NAPERVILLE, ILLINOIS

Published by Sourcebooks, Inc.
P.O. Box 4410, Naperville, Illinois 60567-4410
(630) 961-3900
FAX: (630) 961-2168
www.sourcebooks.com

Library of Congress Cataloging-in-Publication Data

McGovern, Robert J. (Robert John)
  Bring your "A" game : the 10 career secrets of the high achiever / Robert J.
McGovern.
    p. cm.
  Includes index.
  ISBN 1-4022-0516-3 (alk. paper)
  1. Career development. I. Title.

HF5381.M39628 2005
650.1--dc22

                                                    2005016585

Printed and bound in Canada.
WC 10 9 8 7 6 5 4 3 2 1

To Grant and Meghan.
Dad loves you more than words can say.

Table of Contents

Acknowledgments

This book would not have been possible without the help of five extraordinary women.

My wife, Nancy, was a patient and encouraging force throughout the two years that it took to undertake this project. She had already established herself as a great partner in my executive, entrepreneurial, and parenting endeavors and she can now add this book to our list of joint accomplishments. From helping to pick titles, to keeping the kids out of the study as Dad suffered through another round of writer's block, she was always there.

My editor, Tracy Quinn McLennan, was a dream partner for this first-time author. She played the roles of cheerleader, taskmaster, researcher, editor, fellow Red Sox fan, and good friend each and every day we've been a team. When I first hired Tracy as my editor I sent her a copy of an early manuscript. After a few days I called her for a reaction, and hearing her hesitation I sheepishly asked if any of the 50,000 words were salvageable. Her answer: "Of course; they're just all in the wrong order." Tracy, thanks for helping me get it right. This book is as much yours as it is mine.

Two of my former employees helped me formulate my thoughts and hone the focus of the book. Kate Dawson, my friend and favorite idea person, helped me with research and content. My friend, Laura Boswell, a very talented freelance writer and a cool person, was a great sounding board. She also helped me find the courage to take on this formidable undertaking.

Lastly, I am the product of a very talented entrepreneur. My mother, Shirley, was born into a fatherless family in the inner city of Philadelphia. She never completed high school yet somehow managed to become a very successful real estate business owner. She did this while raising three kids as a single mother. There has never been a day in my life when I haven't felt her guiding and sometimes nudging hands behind me saying, "You can do it; anything is possible." Somehow saying thank you just doesn't seem enough.

Introduction

Before I begin giving you advice about your career, it's only fair that I tell you a bit about mine. In 1983, the summer after I graduated college, I embarked on a year-long training program to become a sales engineer with the Hewlett-Packard Company at their Palo Alto, California campus. To say that I was feeling inferior is a huge understatement. The name tags worn by the other students confirmed my worst fears: almost everyone in the class was from a prestigious school like Harvard, MIT, Stanford, or Berkeley. Hewlett-Packard has long been affiliated with top-tier schools; their corporate headquarters are *on* Stanford's campus. I, on the other end of the spectrum, had just graduated from a public university with an undergraduate degree in business administration, and I was sure I was the token state school kid in the class. I only made it there for one reason: I was a co-op student at IBM during my senior year and had gained experience working with computers. HP was trying to transform itself into a computer company, and there were few of us around back then who had actual hands-on experience.

All of my fears were amplified as I sat in the auditorium. Waiting for the class to begin, I observed that many people seemed to know each other. It was my first lesson in the old boys' network. The second lesson came during the first presenter's talk. He made an off-hand joke about UC Berkeley engineers—clearly he was one of the Stanford guys—that drew raves from his fellow alumni. In the back of my mind, I was saying a private prayer that they wouldn't be collecting SAT scores.

Throughout the first week of training it was clear that these were special people; they dressed better, studied more efficiently, asked better questions, and even paid attention better than any student I'd shared a classroom with. If you were to make a wager on who would be successful in the class, I doubt you would have placed a bet on me. These were some of the most impressive people from the best schools in the country. It was their destiny to succeed.

Your bet would have paid off handsomely during the next few years as we launched our careers. In the early-going, these prestigious alumni connections and contacts helped them find plum positions—which meant better exposure, which led to a faster start. And then a funny thing started to happen. An invisible force seemed to even things out. Their auspicious starts were no more promising than mine.

When I look back and think about my peers, friends, former employees, and contacts who were loosely in my age group, there didn't seem to be a correlation between how much ivy grew on their schools and their success. Sure, they got a great education, but something else was determining whether these people succeeded or failed in their career mission. For most of my career I've been busy building successful teams, organizations, and businesses, and all the while this achievement gap has grown into a sort of obsession. If it's not education, what makes people successful? What makes the superstar tick? You'll find those answers here, in this book.

But let me backtrack. The first eighteen years of my career went something like this. For ten years I rose through the ranks of Hewlett-Packard, both in the U.S. and Europe. From there, at the age of thirty-three, I went to work for a mid-sized software firm as general manager of a $200 million, 200-person division, where I learned how to run my own business unit without the safety net of a large corporation. I participated in the sale of that company, which went to our largest competitor, for $2 billion. At age thirty-five I started my own company, CareerBuilder, eventually employing 400 people and earning $145 million in revenues. CareerBuilder is now the Internet's largest career site, with more than fifteen million visitors per month. After a seven year company-building effort, I sold CareerBuilder to two of the nation's largest media companies in transactions valued at several hundred million dollars.

If I sound like a fast-tracker, I'm not. I'm actually a plodder by nature. I drive my golf partners nuts by never winning any driving contests but always keeping the ball in play, one shot at a time. So how does a plodder like me beat countless prestige-university grads to the finish line? By taking my career one day—and one skill—at a time, with a steady and patient view of my final objective.

Throughout my career, I have derived tremendous pleasure from helping others with *their* careers. CareerBuilder's name and mission are not coincidental; I started the company because I like helping others get ahead in life. Before the Internet, the universe of available jobs was a big mystery, and I was determined to change that. Believe it or not, in the "old days" (the prehistoric days we now call "pre-Internet") there was no way to tell if a company was hiring, what benefits they offered, or where they had offices. The process was completely blind: find the address of a company at your local library, send in your résumé, and pray something happened. By creating a frictionless career marketplace, CareerBuilder was designed to help millions of job seekers and thousands of companies find each other in ways that weren't possible doing things the old way. Truthfully, I wrote this book in an effort to help you maximize your life's work. While I don't profess to know everything, I think I've figured a few things out—which I'd like to share with you over the course of these pages.

So, let's get back to the superstar. It's my belief that there are common attributes to be found among people in their mid-thirties with blossoming careers. Most often the seeds of this success were sown in their twenties, during the formative part of their careers. In other words, the success we are observing in the hotshot executive as she arrives at prime time in her career is a result of things she was doing in the first ten years of her career. If you log onto Amazon.com you'll find scores of books designed to fix, patch, salvage, or restructure a midlife career gone wrong. This book is about doing things right the first time, in the early phases of your career. If you do, you'll be too busy to know or care about the latest trendy new career fix-it book when you're thirty-five.

If I were sitting in your shoes, I admit that my bullshit detector would be sounding its alarm. I'd be saying to myself: what the heck does this guy know, and why should I listen to him? Both are fair questions. If my experience doesn't convince you, I can tell you that I might be the world's biggest skeptic; thus, I'm an unlikely candidate to write a waste-of-time book.

We all have developed strengths and weaknesses, and I believe one of my core strengths is my curiosity. I have a deep-rooted need to know how things work, which has me in a constant state of observation. Whether it's understanding how a new technology works or why a bright young person is heads and shoulders above his peers, I enjoy figuring things out. My intent with this book is to loan you the output of this curiosity for a few hours.

By summarizing the observations I've made about young achievers and their workplace performance, I believe I can help you learn from their successes. At CareerBuilder, the majority of my employees were twenty-somethings. The company was even once described as a Generation X hangout run by five "adults." I've managed and coached hundreds of young people, and I believe I've had a pretty good vantage point by which to make these observations.

When I was in college, I remember reading my business textbooks with intense skepticism. It didn't take me long to realize that most textbooks were written by college professors, and the professors I was meeting had never spent any real time in a company. I told myself that if I ever wrote a book I'd make sure it was from a real-world perspective, based on real experiences. And that's what you are going to find on these pages. I'm going to tell you about real-world lessons, and whenever possible, with the exception of changing their names, real people in real work situations. The overall goal of the book is to get you thinking. It's not designed to be a quick-fix but rather an introspective journey of personal improvement. You may find some of the advice immediately helpful, although I'd be just as happy if a concept from the book comes to mind three years from now when you're facing a difficult situation.

So this is a from-the-trenches perspective; this book results from my day-to-day experiences in the workplace, building organizations and companies. I'm not an academic turned workplace expert, so if this doesn't sound like PhD-speak, it's for good reason. I'm fully prepared for you to conclude after reading this book that it didn't have the most eloquent prose, but I hope you'll say that it was at all times real-world, useful, and believable. In the following pages we're going to dissect the attributes of the star performer with an eye towards giving you the opportunities to incorporate new approaches to furthering your own career. The goal is simple and worthy: to give you a leg-up in the challenge of achieving your dreams and aspirations. Together, we're going to make a great team. Let's get to it.

Part One

The Building Blocks of a Successful Career

Why don't they pass a constitutional amendment prohibiting
anybody from learning anything? If it works as well as
Prohibition did, in five years Americans
would be the smartest race of people on Earth.

—*Will Rogers (1879–1935), U.S. humorist and actor*

Chapter 1

Let the Good Times Roll

Prosperity is just around the corner.

—Herbert Hoover (1874-1964), 31st president of the U.S.
(The Dow Jones Industrial Average is up 28,590 percent
since he made that speech.)

When the history books of the early twenty-first century are written, this time may be viewed as one of the most employee favorable periods, ever. Our economy is approaching a period of unprecedented opportunity for young people like you. *It's our mission as a team, to make sure we maximize the remaining days in your career's formative period, with a goal of making you well-positioned for this prosperous time.* If we do the right things, you'll find yourself a rare and valued commodity. Incidentally, I fully expect that most of your peers will miss this opportunity—mainly because they are unwillingly to make the personal development commitment that a successful career requires. Personal growth takes an immense amount of emotional maturity and commitment. Simply put, it's hard work. While most people give it lip service, the number of people who are willing to back up their words with action is small. The fact that you picked up this book is a good sign; it demonstrates your commitment to improving yourself and your career prospects.

A short history refresher may help to demonstrate why we're at the tip of a very prosperous period. America was enjoying tremendous economic success that came with the end of World War II. One of the byproducts of this period of economic prosperity was a higher than normal birthrate, often referred to as the Baby Boom. There were 68 million people born between 1950 and 1966, making up the Baby Boom generation. During the subsequent eighteen-year period, from 1967 to 1981, there were 55 million people born into Generation X. I've done the math for you: there are thirteen million *fewer* Generation X'ers than Baby Boomers.

Baby Boomers entered the workforce in the early 1970s and will begin retiring in 2014. In many instances, they hold the senior positions in their organizations, such as senior manager, head nurse, business owner, chief pilot, or senior partner. Now let me ask you a question. Who do you think is going to replace these people as they exit the workforce? If you guessed Generation X (and let's not forget Generation Y, those born between 1982 and 1995), you're one for one.

The best and brightest from your generation have big shoes to fill. While many of your peers will get their acts together too late to benefit from this demographic trend, it's your job to make sure you're ideally positioned to surf this wave.

Let's also keep in mind what you learned in Economics 101 about supply and demand. Remember that there are only 55 million people in your generation available to fill 68 million jobs. When demand outpaces supply, prices go up. In this case, the expected shortfall of workers foreshadows higher salaries. We've seen this phenomenon happen a countless number of times within specific professions. For the past few decades, software professionals, teachers, and nurses have been in short supply; thus, they have been enjoying pay raises that outpace the overall rate of inflation. Similarly, when the business magazines were talking about record enrollment in medical schools during the 1980s, it resulted in an overabundance of doctors in the 90s, leading to lower incomes. Simple concept but one well worth keeping in mind.

The "A" Player's Top 10 Skill Set

So who are the likely winners in this bright economic future? What skills do they possess that will make them come out on top?

It's tempting to chalk-up a person's success to one or two killer attributes. We often hear: *He's got the gift of gab; She's an adroit inter-company politician; He's a scientific wiz kid;* or *She's a real visionary.* We try to distill the achiever down to his special sauce. The reality is that most successful career achievers do many things well, with the whole package contributing to their meteoric success. For years I have observed a level of consistency in the ingredients of successful people. They all seem to learn how to do a short list of critical things in their first ten years, with the payoff coming in their thirties, forties, and fifties. Before I start the drum roll, I should tell you that I haven't seen any evidence that these are innate skills. They all seem to be acquired the old-fashioned way—through learning, mistakes, and refinement.

So what do people who bring their "A" games to the table every day do that's different than the rest of us? What makes them so special? Most of them possess many, if not all, of the following:

1. A formal, self-developed career plan.

They realize that perspiration and inspiration are not enough. They can tell you their ideal next job, and the one after that, because with the overall objective in mind, intermediate planning becomes second nature.

2. The ability to do the easy stuff well.

They manage to avoid the pitfalls that trip up the brightest and most promising people. The easy stuff isn't mentioned on an annual performance evaluation, although it only takes one or two failings in this area to sidetrack potential stars.

3. A willingness to be coached.

They're open and enthusiastic to feedback that will help them improve themselves and their career prospects. They use special techniques that make their managers *want* to work to see them succeed.

4. An action-oriented curiosity.

Never content to let a potential learning experience escape their grasp, they have well-honed techniques for acquiring workplace knowledge.

5. The ability to communicate clearly.

When they speak, people listen. It's not because they have the loudest voice or the most persistent nagging skills. They live by a few key rules that allow them to get their points across in a manner that is digestible and respected by their colleagues.

6. Superior people skills.

They know how to deal with people on a level that goes beyond the superficial. By using empathetic techniques, they develop better interaction skills that span their conversations, negotiations, and relationships.

7. The ability to handle corporate combat.

Career achievers realize the fundamental purpose of an organization is to create something that is more capable than its individuals acting independently. They know how to grow, prosper, and contribute within the bounds of the company—despite difficulties with individuals who surround them.

8. The ability to learn by observation.

The career achievers learn how to develop a virtual team of people who can teach them core soft skills. Their mentors and role models allow them to assemble a "best of" collection of skills and techniques.

9. Resourceful problem solving skills.

Never content to let a problem go unsolved, they come up with novel approaches to solving difficult problems—and earn their managers' and peers' respect in doing so.

10. The ability to make sound career choices.

A career in its purest form is a collection of choices related to how you want to spend the waking hours of your life. The superstars have developed techniques for making logical, fact-based career decisions that correspond with their overall plans.

Over the course of this book, we'll discuss these skill areas, helping you focus on how defining and acquiring (or reinforcing) your skill set will help you execute the ultimate plan for your future. And because careers, like life, follow meandering paths, and a winding road that often leads to dead ends, you'll find a section of emergency procedures that shows you how to step back and redirect your path if at any point along the way you encounter a setback. In these emergency procedure chapters, we'll deal specifically with three issues: losing your job, getting out of a career rut, and learning to love what you do.

Stairway to Nowhere

Most people attack their career vertically, climbing the proverbial ladder. If you're trying to build a tall structure, going straight up isn't always the best solution. Tall structures need a solid platform and adequate lateral support to stabilize their height. In a career context, a person with an approach that's too vertical often finds he's not sufficiently rounded or resilient as he progresses upward.

Here's an example: let's take the case of a person who wants to be the CEO of the company one day. He develops what he believes to be the shortest path to the corner office:

he's going to start in sales and rapidly progress through a series of promotions until he reaches his objective. Using vertical blocks, it might look something like this:

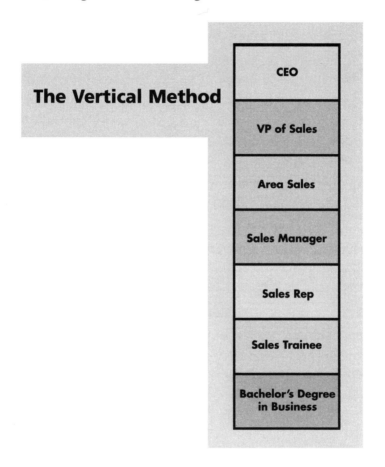

The Vertical Method

CEO

VP of Sales

Area Sales

Sales Manager

Sales Rep

Sales Trainee

Bachelor's Degree in Business

Now let's talk about the challenges of this approach. With a vertical orientation, this person is by default defining himself as a specialist. Let's say the company sells digital photographic equipment. In his plan he's an expert, with ever-increasing sales management skills. Now let's envision a few realistic and likely obstacles he'll face. With such specialization, what's going to happen to this guy once the digital photography revolution peters out? His résumé is going to read "digital photography sales expert," which might be as marketable as a candle maker in today's context. Suppose his company converts to a different sales model in which outside selling skills are no longer required. Is he prepared to do anything else in the company? Doubtful. How about the risk that he'll fall short of his overall objective? The CEO candidate for this company must manage all these company functions and needs a broad array of skills, including finance, marketing, accounting, sales, and manufacturing. If you were a shareholder, would you want a one-dimensional salesperson heading *your* company? Doubtful again.

The best approach to developing and executing a career plan is to take a platform approach, assembling your experiences and attributes into a more stable and resilient pyramid shape. The first phase of your career is focused on building a solid platform of experiences that will create a foundation that will last, despite your job title. It's also the time during which you can acquire as many of the "A" player's top ten skills as possible. Why? Because you'll probably never make it to the maximization phase of your career without a critical mass of these core skills. Here's what the skills pyramid could look like for someone whose goal is to be a senior partner in a large accounting firm:

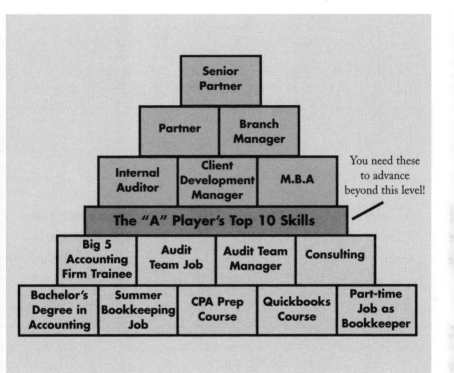

Bring Your "A" Game will show you how to assemble these skills and experiences for your own career.

In Chapter 2 we'll take a closer look at the skills pyramid and lay the groundwork for building your own solid foundation for career success.

Chapter 2
Your Skills Pyramid

Go confidently in the direction of your dreams.
Live the life you have imagined.

—Henry David Thoreau (1817–1862),
American essayist, poet, and philosopher

I know quite a few people who made premature grabs for the brass ring—and ended up flat on their backs on the mat. One guy left a great career in corporate finance to join a multi-level marketing scheme just as it was imploding. Another saw future earnings totaling millions of dollars in the promising world of auditing corporate electric bills for mistakes—only to see the reality earnings in the mere hundreds. They bolted for the next big thing, whether it was artificial intelligence, Nu Skin, or day trading. During the dot-com bubble, everyone wanted their piece of the pie, which led to too many career failures to count. If these people were Olympic divers, they'd be the contestants trying to accomplish the never-before-tried quadruple back summersault reverse entry dive. From a distance, the odds look better for a belly flop than a gold medal, but somehow they become blinded by the opportunity and jump. If I had been their coach, I would stop them right before the dive and whisper a secret in their ear: "It's also possible to score a perfect 10 with the well-executed swan dive." It's true—you can win a gold medal with a graceful and uncomplicated swan dive. *Most "A" players are doing a daily version of the corporate swan dive. They set achievable goals and back them up with sound execution.* It's not flashy or outwardly exciting, but it's the path to the corner office.

Few complex goals achieve successful completion without a sound plan of attack and some preparation. You'd be crazy to run a marathon if you hadn't been training for months. You wouldn't take the bar exam without having attended law school. You'd probably not plan a $100,000 wedding without having a fiancé.

A career may be one of the most complex projects you'll ever undertake. It's a forty-five-year-long strategy game with constantly changing rules and protracted outcomes. Tougher still, the tactics you employ in the first ten years of the game may take twenty or thirty years to validate. Your career will be composed of countless decisions that have neither right nor wrong answers, but all have the potential of affecting your financial security and self-worth in the long- and short-term. And not to add any more heat to the pressure cooker—the first ten years of one's career can often be the "make it or break it" period. Worse still, being successful in your career does not necessarily equate with simply working hard. Sadly, there are a lot of people putting in seventy-hour weeks and not getting ahead in their jobs. They feel like they are putting their hearts and souls into their careers without the recognition, rewards, and advancement they think they deserve. Rather than relying on hard work—or long hours—alone, it's healthier to say that *we can accomplish our goals if we have a sound plan coupled with a willingness to work hard at executing it.*

You may be one of those people who has already reaped the benefits of implementing and seeing through a long-range plan. It may have begun back in high school when you decided your major for college and where you would continue your education. You may have gone on to complete post-graduate studies as well. You may also have participated in internships, co-ops, and residencies to give you real-life work experience.

You think that all the preparation is behind you now, right? Nope. Much like you have been doing since your teenage years, you need to continue with the education and learning experiences that will enable you to map out the steps for a winning career plan.

On the other hand, you may be less of a fast-tracker and haven't had much success implementing and carrying out long-range plans. Whatever your history, you're now ready to take the first steps for your long-term future. Together, we'll map out a rough template to guide your career, including the educational moves you'll need to make up—and across—your career pyramid.

Why a Plan Is Crucial

Consider this: a human life is about 26,000 days. If you think that sounds like a small number, bear in mind that a forty-five-year career works out to only about 10,000 days. How you plan and execute a strategy to maximize these precious days will determine whether you'll achieve early retirement at age fifty, or will be working to supplement your Social Security at seventy. Retirement in Boca or Baltimore, funding your child's college education, or saddling him with pile of student loans—*it will all come down to the quality of your career plan.*

Contemplating your own retirement or funding a college education for your unborn son when you're in your twenties and thirties might seem like a foreign thought. You may even be thinking: "I haven't paid off my own college bills and he wants me thinking about the children I don't even have." Fair enough…but there's a worthy "but" to consider. There are substantial near-term rewards to be realized along the path to a successful career, an upgrade from a cube to an office, achieving true financial independence that makes you immune to the vagaries of economic and corporate cycles, and waking up every day with a strong sense of motivation and enthusiasm are some of the perks that come with a rise to the top. A career can be an awesomely fun and stimulating endeavor.

When constructing a career plan, it's important to accurately gauge the available time to complete each element of the plan. Here's an example. Suppose at a relatively young age you decided that you wanted to be an astronaut. Let's say that you sat down on your fifteenth birthday to lay out a plan to help you achieve your goal of soaring through the heavens. Your plan would include important elements like completing high school with a high grade point average, graduating from college with a degree in a scientific or technological field, attaining a private pilot's license by your nineteenth birthday, joining a military pilot program, maintaining excellent health and fitness, etc. Graphically, your plan would appear as a pyramid of blocks, each marked with a particular life experience or skill that would contribute to your ultimate success. It would look something like this:

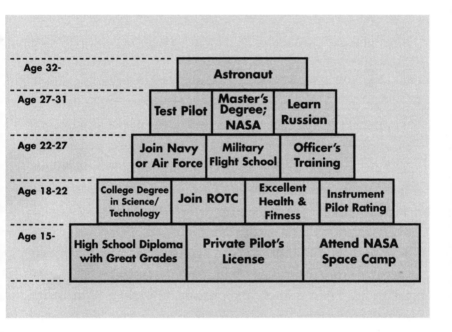

While not a slam dunk, your plan gives you a good shot at achieving your goal. Now, consider the important role that time plays in this plan. Let's say when you were twenty-nine-years-old you decided that you wanted to be an astronaut. You had been working for eight years in the banking industry. Could you put together a pyramid of steps that would lead you to that outcome? I'd say your odds would be pretty long, particularly because you would probably be shut out from key elements like joining the military and attaining officer's training.

Although it's a dramatic example, most professions work in a similar way. Advancement in nearly every career starts with planning steps that start surprisingly early in life. And, over time, one's tactical agility diminishes due to the written or unwritten prerequisites of a particular industry or job. Whether you want to be an Olympic athlete, a software programmer, a high school principal, or vice president in a bank, it's helpful to know this objective sooner rather than later.

Just in case you're reading this and saying "Yeah, but…," we should address the career moonshots—people who lead us to conclude anything is plausible. You know, people like Michael Dell who started a computer company in his dorm and became a billionaire in his twenties. You probably hear tales of a legendary alum from your college who was a late bloomer but found a great career track at thirty-years-old— after backpacking through Asia for five years. While it's true that anything's possible, it's important to remember that some things are more possible than others. Question: How many successful, affluent, and satisfied people are there who followed a deliberate, focused, and patient career progression? Answer: Millions. Question: How many Michael Dell moonshots are there? Answer: A few each decade. If you're thinking, "Yeah, but…," remember swan dives.

The very successful careers of high achievers tend to conform to a predictable set of phases. In their twenties, high achievers are focused primarily on learning. They are acquiring the fundamental skills and techniques that will serve as a platform for their entire career. With this solid foundation, they can then enter their thirties positioned to apply these life lessons and gain a defined career trajectory. The higher the quality of the lessons, the steeper the career trajectory. It's also the time when most successful people enter a period of accelerated financial returns because they are receiving fair value for their skills. The forties are a period of financial maximization—cashing in on the progress made in the twenties and thirties. If you've done everything right, your fifties will be an exciting time when you're raking in the rewards of your career planning efforts. Whether your dream is to retire early in your beachfront home or to devote the second half of your life to a non-profit cause you're passionate about, this outcome will largely depend on the quality the things you do in your twenties and thirties.

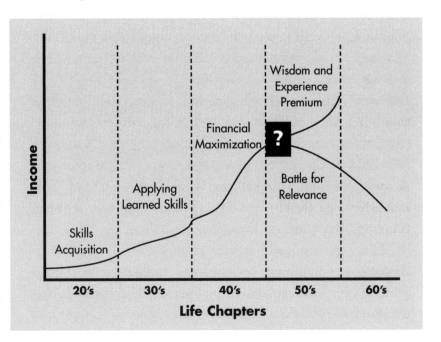

Constructing Your Plan

Remember, it's wise not to think of your career in the form of a ladder, but as a pyramid of blocks each representing the major educational, skill development, and growth experiences that will make up your career. If you have ever played with Lego blocks, you know that sometimes you have to build across, or even down, before you can build a higher structure. And, as with all structures, in order to build higher you must ensure that each successive level can serve as a strong platform for what will be built above it. To make things interesting, your pyramid has obstacles and time pressures associated with certain blocks. For example, completing college in your early twenties is much more desirable than in your forties.

The most important step in the process is to define the Top box in your pyramid. Without a clearly defined project goal or Top box, it's nearly impossible to do an adequate job building the underlying superstructure of the pyramid. In contrast, with an end goal in mind, we can get surprisingly precise in planning the learning steps and associated career moves that will contribute to your success.

At this point you are probably asking yourself: "Does this guy really expect me to know where I want to be twenty or thirty years from now?" Well, that depends. If you want to have a middling career that evolves through happenstance, you could probably just keep doing what you are doing. Time and inertia are the enemy of the career plan. Just like the master chess player, you need to keep one eye on the decision clock.

One of the sad growing older experiences I have had is watching some of my friends get trapped in a fight for relevance in the mid- to late-parts of their careers. While they had intentions of staying where they are, they eventually found themselves replaced by younger, more enthusiastic people who could do their jobs at a much lower salary. It all amounts to a lose-your-job situation when the contribution or benefit you bring to the business doesn't measure up to your salary. It's sad but true that middle-age workers often find themselves in this quandary when their perceived worth doesn't balance with their relatively high salary. Workers in their fifties often find themselves in a tumultuous period. The successful person sits at the fulcrum of two economic forces: being valued for their experience and wisdom versus the potential of being replaced by a more youthful and less expensive person. *Your job is to make yourself one of the most valuable commodities in the economy. Because we are all living in an increasingly up-or-out world, we need to be focused on growth and skills building right up to our retirement parties.*

SWM ISO Career Utopia

Many people have a belief there's this great but elusive career they just haven't yet discovered. Rather than putting a stake in the ground in a particular profession or industry, they cast about in entry-level positions with the hope that a bolt of lightning hits them with the great plan. The job that pays very well, involves very interesting and exciting work in a stress-free environment, at a company everyone respects and admires. It's the job that will make your friends say, "That's such a cool job!" Does it ever happen this way? Of course—in Tom Cruise movies. Yes, it's important to work in an industry that you find interesting. No, you shouldn't waste time casting about trying to find that true love match between you and the perfect profession since it rarely happens that way. The truth is, most successful people fall in love with their profession and industry over time, as opposed to being hit with Cupid's career arrow. Every industry, profession, and job has ups and downs, rewards and hassles, and opportunities to succeed and fail. You'd be smart to not waste your time trying to find utopia.

Incidentally, it seems there is an inverse relationship to salary and attractiveness of an industry. Glitzy industries—like sports, entertainment, and travel—tend to pay poorly, perhaps because there are so many people who are chasing so few opportunities. As a general rule of thumb, life on the other side of the supply and demand curve is generally more lucrative.

Defining Your Worth: The Personal Value Formula

Your career pyramid is another way of correlating your personal worth to the overall economy. In an ideal world, you'd like to be on an ever-increasing path to raising your value on the economic playing field. Just like the star quarterback or the proven turnaround specialist CEO, you want your services to result in a growing demand for an increasingly higher price. Here's a formula that marketers use to quantify the value of a product or service:

$$\text{Value} = \text{Benefits} - \text{Price}$$

This equation says that in a rational economy, the value attributed to a person, product, or service will be the sum of all the perceived benefits minus its perceived cost. Keep in mind the importance of the word "perceived" in this definition, as perceived benefits and price can take all different forms. If a person requires both a high salary and a high level of tolerance to put up with his whining, then his "price" might not outweigh his benefits. I once had an employee who was excellent at his job, but his penchant for telling off-color jokes and making inappropriate comments led to his demise. The price of putting up with all of his coworkers' complaints to the HR department outweighed the wizardry he could perform on our corporate network.

The thing to keep in mind is that a corporation is about the most rational entity that's ever been conceived. You can always count on a company to do what is in its best financial interests. In fact, if you look the articles of incorporation, which is the document that legalistically describes the company's mission, 99.9 percent of the time the purpose of the company is to maximize shareholder value. In other words, make its shareholders rich through increasing profits. And what's the most rational thing this economic organism can do? Hire and retain great people at a reasonable cost. When we used to talk about a company's assets, we described their factories. Now, in our post-industrial economy, we say that the company's assets drive home every night. The workforce is just a big ecosystem that rewards smart, skilled people who know where they want to go.

Who Do You Want to Be When You Grow Old?

Here's an exercise for you that should help you fill in your Top box. Sit back and imagine that you're at your own funeral. This isn't a sad occasion but rather a happy celebration of what turned out to be your wonderful life. Play the tape in your mind. All of your friends and family have gathered to remember your time on earth. Everyone in attendance is both sad and happy—sad, of course that you're gone but happy that you had a full, rewarding, and satisfying life. As the clergywoman is reading your eulogy, she says, "He was a great husband, a loving son, a devoted father, and _____." Now, think for a moment. What would you have liked her to say about your life's work? How would you fill in that blank?

Ideally the clergywoman would have described the Top box in your pyramid. How would she have described your life's work? Did she say you were a wealthy self-made entrepreneur turned philanthropist? A corporate executive? A member of Congress? Make it a point to spend time thinking about how you would answer this question. I have a friend who thinks you aren't a complete person until you can name the three things you'd like accomplish while you're on this earth. Can you name yours?

Another spin on the exercise is to imagine writing your own obituary. Would yours be a standard newspaper death announcement or would it be a three-column article with a photo detailing all the great things you'd achieved with your life? You don't want to have the summation of your life be a one-inch box of three sentences that every funeral home contributes to their local papers, do you?

The Top Box

Let's construct an example to illustrate how the answer to the question of what you want in your Top box can affect the overall construction of your pyramid. Let's fill in the blank to say Retail Store Owner, and in order to have a precise example, we'll say you wanted a start a new type of pet store. It's a pet supply superstore that you'd like to expand into a small chain of stores. We'll use this to illustrate a thought process, although you'll find it a generic approach that can be used with your true-to-life answer.

You'd probably want to start your thought process by thinking about what it would take to be a successful entrepreneur. Many people think that becoming a business owner is a process that begins when a person suddenly says, "I'm sick of this life working for someone else and it's time to strike out on my own." The popular press loves to glorify the story in which someone cashes it all in, takes a big risk—maybe even leverages their credit cards to the hilt—and creates a company like Starbucks or Amazon. What the story often leaves out is that the entrepreneur who founded the company spent years preparing for this calculated moment. In the case of Starbucks, Howard Shultz, the company's founder, rose through the ranks of Xerox and Hammerplast, ultimately running U.S. operations for the Hammerplast global consumer products conglomerate. With Amazon, Jeff Bezos rose through the ranks of Bankers Trust, becoming the company's youngest V.P. Later, at D.E. Shaw, he was the company's youngest senior vice president. I'll submit to you that the vast majority of successful entrepreneurs didn't just say "the hell with it; I'm sick of my job," but rather they consciously, or subconsciously, built an impressive skills pyramid that dramatically improved their chances of success. Their path was one where they afforded themselves successive life lessons aimed at making them as well-prepared as possible to some day strike out on their own. Perhaps their true genius was having the smarts to learn on their former employer's nickel.

It's often said that 90 percent of all new businesses fail in the first year or two. When you look at the résumés of the typical founder, it's no wonder this is the case. Most people who strike out on their own are poorly prepared for the world they are about to enter. Being successful at this level requires experiences that equip you with the skills, tools, wisdom, and lessons—including mistakes—that will ensure that you aren't operating with a learner's permit in a game that requires professional skills. A good mental backstop is to constantly remind yourself that your competitor will most likely be someone with an impressive skills pyramid. A poorly prepared person quickly learns the true definition of the word *stress*.

So, how would a person who wants to become an entrepreneur in retail plan his ideal skills pyramid? We would start this planning process much like we did for the astronaut exercise. As a helpful tip, create a hypothetical position as your benchmark. For this purpose, let's use an imaginary investor as your benchmark. Chances are you're going to need to raise bank debt or friends and family money to start or expand your enterprise in the future. Ask yourself this question: "If an investor was evaluating a loan to me, a new retailer, what experiences would he be looking for my background?"

There are tens, if not hundreds, of thousands of people who know how to manage a store, but very few are qualified to start one from the ground up. While knowing something about animals would be important to owning a pet store, there are other attributes that make for a successful retail entrepreneur. A prospective investor would most likely want to see you have experience developing products or company strategies, running a profit and loss area, understanding the retail sales domain, demonstrating that you are good at recruiting and hiring good people, and possess knowledge in the financial area in a public or private company. He'd probably also like to see that you're an effective leader of organizations of relatively the same size as what your business plan indicates yours will be in a few years. As you can see, an investor isn't going to be interested in issuing you a learner's permit. Rather, he need to be sure that you've got what it takes to be a good steward of his money and build a great company for your mutual benefit.

Now, let's try mapping it out to see if the plan is viable. Let's say that you are twenty-seven-years-old, with a goal of starting your business by the time you are thirty-eight; which would be prime time in your career. With today's decision, your pyramid might look like this:

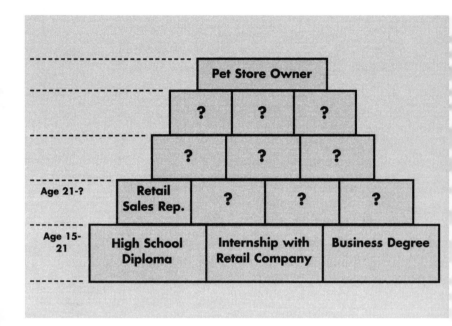

It's a good start, but we've got to figure out a way to help you gain the following experiences that are missing from your start-up founder destiny:

1. Profit and Loss Responsibilities
2. Retail Store Management
3. Financial and Capital Markets
4. Management and Leadership
5. Strategic Planning

Your job over the next eleven years will be to seek out jobs and opportunities that will allow you to fill in these building blocks. Keep in mind that your new and primary objective is to prepare you for your life as an entrepreneur. Perhaps it would look something like this:

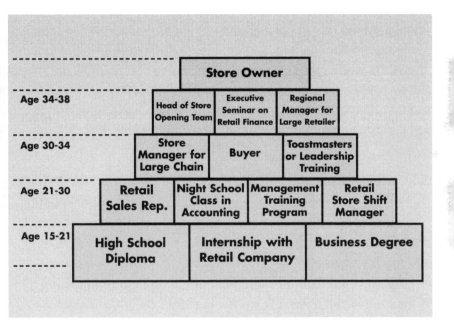

Remember that one of the keys to your success will be to remain committed and true to your plan. Along the way you'll most likely be asked to entertain offers that might provide short-term benefit. These offers may come in the form of a friend who starts a business or a former boss who wants you to join her. It's important that you evaluate every job opportunity in the context of what you will learn in that position. When people take dead-end jobs, it's most often because they lose sight of the overall picture. You'll find that this potential distraction effect will grow over time since the pursuit of your pyramid will naturally make you more valuable, thus, drawing attention from nearby observers, like friends and former and prospective employers. In fact, I'll be surprised if you aren't fighting off short-term opportunities along the way. In other words, it might not be the shortest path to a director title, but it may be the only path to a vice president or CEO title. While your peers will constantly be looking for that career-making, homerun promotion, you'll now be more focused on hitting the singles and doubles that will lead to a hall-of-fame career. You will be surprised at how much more you will enjoy your career, once you can put each day into the context of your overall plan. Perhaps you'll find yourself in a situation where your company is implementing significant financial cutbacks. Your new perspective will be: I'm really going to pay attention to how the senior managers communicate and roll-out these cuts since I might have to do this myself someday. Or, maybe you'll be assigned to work on a difficult and undesirable customer account. While yesterday you might have looked at this as the equivalent of being sent to Siberia, now you'll tell yourself that the start-up CEO is the chief customer satisfaction officer; this assignment might give you a chance to hone your difficult people skills. You can now put every challenge, assignment, and opportunity into context by asking yourself, "What will I learn?" and "How can use this to further my goal of being _____?"

To access online tools about building your skills pyramid, visit my website at www.mkt10.com. Now, let's start creating your Top box!

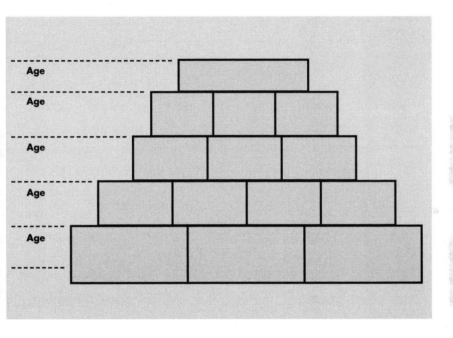

Chapter 3

What's in Your Top Box?

The person who makes a success of living is the one
who sees his goal steadily and aims for it unswervingly.
That is dedication.

—Cecil B. DeMille (1881–1959),
American motion picture producer and director

Someone once asked Wayne Gretzky, the greatest hockey
player who ever lived, about the secrets to his success.
Without hesitation, he replied, "Everyone else skates to the
puck; I skate to where the puck is going to be." Gretzky's goal-
scoring prowess earned him the nickname "The Great One,"
which he attributes to the simple act of anticipating where he
needed to be on the ice, at the right time. You should use that
thinking for your Top box in your career pyramid. It's
imperative that you skate to where the opportunities are *going
to be* versus where they *are* today.

I'm not asking you to hone psychic abilities so you can
predict the future—thankfully it's easier than that. Think
about it this way: the vast majority of the jobs that you can

name today probably didn't exist twenty-five years ago. There's almost zero chance that a high school guidance counselor would have directed students in 1979 into the fields of LAN administrator, Java programmer, or chief technology officer. In a broader context, you wouldn't have come up with MRI technician, telesales executive, or hedge fund manager. Short of being able to see the future, how can we determine where the jobs—and you—need to be?

Take this example. In the 1960s classic movie *The Graduate*, a confused and disillusioned recent college graduate played by Dustin Hoffman reluctantly arrives at a graduation party thrown by his parents. As he is going through the motions of greeting his parents' friends, an obnoxious uncle pulls him aside and says, "Benjamin, you only need to know one word: plastics." Back in the late 1960s, plastic was seen as a new wonder material—much like how we think of the advancements in nano-materials today that are allowing scientists to create a new generation of vastly superior fabrics, plastic solar panels, and airplanes that are faster, lighter, and more fuel efficient than yesterday's largely aluminum airliners. In a world of metal, ceramic, and wood, it was truly an innovation to be able to mold a cup, dashboard, or bike seat into a free form shape. It would have been a prescient move by young Benjamin to enter this new and emerging industry.

So is the idea to be like Benjamin? Pick a hot spot and surf that wave? Well, yes. But you need to be sure to plot a course to intercept a future place in time, ideally when both the opportunity and your economic worth are peaking in unison.

This intercept point is key. Imagine, for example, if in 2005 you were peaking in your chosen profession within computer network security, hydrogen fuel cell engineering, stem cell research, or homeland security. You'd be pulling down a large paycheck with great upside career potential in the early years of a twenty-year trend.

The ultimate manifestation of your forward thinking will be what you put in the Top box in your pyramid. It's the most important block in your plan. The most critical element of this structured thinking is for you to acknowledge that you are trying to intercept a future point in time versus catching up to a stationary target. *In other words, you need to prepare yourself for a future job description instead of one that exists today.* Why?

Occupations That Didn't Exist Thirty Years Ago:

· Network Engineer
· Webmaster
· Telesales
· Java Programmer
· C++ Programmer
· CAD/CAM Designer
· IT Trainer
· Online Marketer
· MRI Technician
· Database Administrator
· Computer Security Expert
· Computer Graphics Designer
· Genetics Scientist

Because the economic landscape is in a constant state of evolution, driven by a constant current of innovation, changing tastes, and societal influences. (For a more comprehensive set of career selection tools, visit www.mkt10.com.)

Now, before you point out that you don't know the first thing about reading a crystal ball, let me add that I haven't seen any evidence that successful people are born with an innate talent to see the future. Instead, I have observed that many high achievers have a self-developed skill that enables them to make good, educated guesses about what comes next. Sometimes we read profiles in business magazines of these people who have "vision." What we are acknowledging is that these people have developed the skill to extrapolate today's trends into a vision for the not-too-distant future. The trends might be a new enabling technology in their industry, the sales results for their latest product, or a significant demographic trend in society.

Let's say that you recently attained a master's degree, either at the beginning of your career or later in life. Now you need to enter the industry and profession in which you'd like to apply your education for the next few decades. Again, your key goal should be to intercept a lucrative future growth area in the employment market, instead of an area that may be hot today but on the downward slide and waning. Perhaps you would focus on serving the leisure time or senior care industries that are sure to benefit from the baby boomer retirement trend. I know of one entrepreneur developing a company named Elder Health, which is creating a whole new approach to the long-term care of people in the last years of their lives. Or maybe you'd choose the emerging genetics industry, which is sure to explode after the recent decoding of the human genome. Would this be high-risk? Only if you think DNA manipulation won't be relevant to our well-being in the coming decades. Seems like a pretty safe bet that fuel cells will play a big role in the future of humankind, which makes them worthy of serious consideration. We've all heard the press reporting incessantly about Moore's Law, named after Gordon Moore at Intel, which simply states that microprocessor speeds double every eighteen months. Perhaps you would focus on the software industry, which will be the benefactor of tomorrow's chips that will make computers twenty-five times faster only five short years from now. The economy is a pretty rational place. The only sure-fire way for an investor to make money is to invest his capital in high growth areas, thus capital flows to the most promising long-term opportunities. This is a good metaphor for your career planning efforts. Just like the investor searching for a promising long-term trend, your job is to find those areas in the economy that will deliver the most attractive returns for your skills.

The point is to encourage you to develop your vision skills. *So the next time you see a totalitarian society fall in favor of democracy, a new technology come along like the Internet, a breakthrough in medical thinking, or a shift in population demographics, you should now ask yourself what it means to your economic playing field and how it fits into the context of the Top box in your pyramid.* Virtually every industry features a persistent drone of wave change—our job is to make you an effective surfer of these trends. Ideally, the Top box of your pyramid will remain constant—because you chose an industry with great long-term prospects—and the adjustments you make along the way relate to individual blocks in your pyramid. For example, if you're in manufacturing and the long-term trend is for your products to be manufactured in South America, then adding a "Learn Spanish" skill block to your pyramid would enhance your long-term prospects. By the way, you'll find that these "visionary" skills will serve you well beyond your career-planning activities. Companies put tremendous value on people who are able to think beyond the here and now. If you want to have a title that begins with "Chief," you'll almost certainly have to demonstrate years-out vision as a prerequisite to getting the job.

Predicting Your Career Future

The next time you're a passenger in the car of someone you think is a bad driver, take a look at their eyes. You'll probably see that the driver has his eyes focused on a point on the road that is very close to the front of the car. The reason he provides a herky-jerky ride is that his vision is too focused on the immediate landscape and not the overall picture. He is reacting to driving situations too late.

The same thing happens to people as they plan their careers when they don't look far enough down the road. In contrast, the driver who provides the smooth and comfortable ride is the one looking way down the road in an effort to pre-empt the need to take abrupt and uncomfortable actions. Airline pilots are trained to do this, which they call "staying ahead of the airplane." Skiers are taught to do a similar thing by focusing their eyes further down the mountain. You need to do the same thing with your career. Make a concerted effort to become sensitive to the major trends that affect your economic playing field—whether they are political, legal, demographic, or technology-based—and then be bold enough to develop your own thesis about the opportunities they present. You'll find that the best opportunities are presented by trends that are both obvious and long-foreseen.

Adopt a problem/solution mindset. The human race has been amazingly effective at solving seemingly intractable problems. An increasingly mobile society turned out to be a very productive spreader of disease and infection—until we invented a new industry called pharmaceuticals and invented solutions named antibiotics and vaccines. The Industrial Revolution was responsible for the word "pollution" entering our lexicon, although today's modern automobile emits 98 percent less noxious gas than your grandmother's 1972 Crown Vic. Not bad for thirty-five years of progress. As China and India rapidly become more westernized, they are rapidly going to put immense pressure on world energy supplies. Think of three billion Chinese and Indians with a new appetite for cars, air conditioning, and modern appliances. Sounds like a problem that's going to create a new industry or two in the search for a solution.

Living the Future in the Present

Back in the late 1970s and early 1980s, many young people had the foresight to realize that the personal computer was going to catalyze a completely new career field. I know because I was one of them. Everyone at my university *knew* that computers were going to be huge in the future. But, for reasons that had do with a social stigma of being looked at as a propeller head, seats in the computer science school were easy to attain. Many of us who were looked upon as the geeks and nerds at our colleges and universities are now among the most successful people in our generation. A few are worth more than $100 million—which now seems like a small price to pay for being nicknamed "geek" in their college fraternity. It's important to remind you that the job titles of the positions these high-earners hold today weren't even invented when they committed themselves to a computer industry path. If these people were filling out pyramids back then, they almost certainly wouldn't have said "chief technology officer" in the Top box, although "high level executive in computers" would have been sufficient to get them started. Similarly, thousands of people took it upon themselves to learn Russian, German, or Chinese when they recognized that the end of the Cold War was going to usher in new economic opportunities in the former socialist block countries. Today, these people command a premium for their language and international business skills, which relate to a trend that was very obvious as it unfolded. China is now the fastest growing economy in the world—and it's a society that seems to have decided that economic warfare is the last important turf battle on our globe. Speaking fluent Chinese could have the effect of super-charging many professions, in much the same way English-speaking Europeans were at an advantage in the 1980s and 90s.

Here's an example to help stimulate your thinking. In 2003 the state of California announced that the majority of its births are to people of Hispanic origin. Think about that for a moment. California, a state with nearly sixty million people, representing the sixth-largest economy in the world, larger than traditional powers like France, Great Britain, and Italy, is on a path to becoming mostly Hispanic. How soon will this be felt in the Californian economy? In five short years, half of every kindergarten class will be Hispanic. In twelve to eighteen years half the music, pizzas, and entry-level cars will be bought by this new majority. And, in twenty-one years, half the new entrants to the workforce will be of Hispanic origin. As a populace, California will be the wealthiest Spanish-speaking place on the planet. It might also be one of the most bilingual economies, in a few short years.

How might this affect your pyramid? If you're in sales, retail, or the services industry, learning to speak Spanish looks like it might become essential. If you plan on owning a restaurant, perhaps learning something about the tastes and preferences of this market segment might be an imperative. If you're in high-tech, Spanish language versions of your products might be required by this emerging market trend. Your job is to think about how future developments pertain to your career and make adjustments accordingly.

Perhaps the only difference between the opportunists I've mentioned and Joe Average is that high achievers have the good sense to look down the road. They didn't take a future thinking course at college, nor do they have a special intuition gene. Their genius is simply training their minds to be a little more observant and taking the time to think about the implications of the macro-level changes they see. If you self-develop this skill, you'll find it almost impossible not to always be thinking about what's coming downstream. As you progress through your life, you're going to encounter successful people who made one or more high-payoff bets on the future that paid off.

Trade Short-Term Financial Gains for Long-Term Success

When I was in the computer industry in the early 1990s, many of the hotshot people left and joined what were called plug-compatible mainframe manufacturers. Companies like Hitachi and Amdahl had created clones of IBM's stalwart mainframe machines with a strategy of competing on best price. Well, they made these moves just as the world was moving to PCs and laptops. What seemed like a grab for the financial brass ring soon turned out to be a classic career quagmire. These recent defectors were now stuck branded as "old mainframe guys" in a market that valued personal computer and server skills. With a little forethought, they might have focused their job search efforts on companies like Dell, Microsoft, or Compaq, all of which were positioned to ride this twenty-year trend. This wasn't black magic at the time: the PC trend was obvious and omnipresent to a minority of people—those with vision. The people that made the jump to mainframe manufacturers were lacking a self-developed thesis about where the market was headed; thus, they ended up down a dead-end career road.

You may need to trade-off short-term financial gains for long-term success. Maximize your lifelong earnings instead of what you are going to make next month or next year. In other words, there's a time for learning and development and a time for financial maximization. If you were building a factory to produce widgets, you would be wise to not take a bunch of shortcuts to maximize next year's results at the expense of future years' income. You need to do the same thing with your career. *Think of your career as your personal money-making factory that you're always building for the long-term.*

Occasionally I have the opportunity to help college seniors decide which job offer to take at the end of the on-campus recruiting season. It's humorous to watch an intelligent soon-to-be grad fretting that his preferred job pays $3,000 less per year. Sadly, more often then not, he takes the higher-paying job, as if the human brain is programmed to always take the larger number. In a career that will hopefully yield $5 million in salary, we are now sadly reduced to talking about making a mistake over $167 per month in after-tax income. Suppose the lower-paying offer was from a company with a better training program and a strong track record for promoting within the company? If it put the grad on a 30 percent higher trajectory, it could increase his lifetime earnings by millions.

Stupid Employee Tricks

Another version of this shortsighted thinking comes under the heading of what I'll call Stupid Employee Tricks. When an employee doesn't respect the fact that his workplace conduct today can have a direct and lasting effect on his lifetime earnings potential, disaster often strikes. Question: What's the net value of a superstar salesperson who consistently blows away his sales quotas? Answer: Countless millions of dollars. Question: Now, what's the NPV of the same salesperson who gets fired for padding his expense account a few hundred bucks? Answer: Potentially zero. If you're counting, that's trading a few million for a few hundred, which is generally a bad deal. The same goes for illicit conduct, including inappropriate office relationships like having an affair with your boss, misuse of company IT resources (e.g. Web surfing and chatting at prohibited sites), aggressive behavior, etc. Remember: protect your lifetime earning potential—next to your loved ones, your most cherished asset isn't in your bank account; it's your lifetime earnings potential.

How to Avoid Going from Boom to Bust

The dot-com bubble illustrates the importance of making good choices when dealing with emerging markets. The fact is that many people did well in the boom by working for companies like Microsoft, Cisco, Amazon, and eBay. And conversely, many people lost their shirts at companies trying to do everything from the heroic to the sublime. The natural questions are: 1.) What can we learn from this? and 2.) What can we do differently the next time? The questions are relevant because you'll live through more booms and bust cycles. Here are a few tips that might help you make the right choice(s) when faced with the next inevitable technology boom:

1. Focus on picks and shovels.

During the great California Gold Rush, very few prospectors actually struck it rich. The greatest amount of new wealth was created by the people selling picks, shovels, and provisions to the miners. This has become a well-known secret among the technology industry veterans. During the PC revolution of the 1980s, among the greatest beneficiaries were the companies selling microprocessor chip-making tools, manufacturing devices, and Silicon Valley land. Similarly, much of the true wealth created during the Internet bubble was delivered to the companies selling computers, software, networking services and equipment, and desks and chairs to the dot-coms.

2. Consider technology.

If you examine the smoldering aftermath of the dot-com crash, you'll find that the true technology companies did better than companies trying to apply other company's technologies. The furniture companies that tried to morph themselves into Internet companies faired very poorly. On the other hand, a higher percentage of the pure technology companies—the ones with unique and novel intellectual property—faired comparatively better.

3. Pick the inevitable few.

During the 1980s, the economy saw a boom similar to the dot-com revolution of the late 1990s. Back then it was driven by the advent of the microprocessor chip, which led to the creation of the personal computer industry. In the 1980s, more than 150 personal computer companies went public on the NASDAQ stock market, although by the end of the decade only a handful were still solvent in 2000. The lesson

> "The failure rate was highest for the start-ups that were Internet bets on a business model. Others, with a large technology component, have often found a way for the company and the technology to forward."
>
> —Peter Currie, a partner in the Silicon Valley office of General Atlantic Partners, a leading venture capital firm (as reported in the New York Times, 10/26/03)

here is that there typically isn't room for every new entrant in the market. The key is to go into these situations saying, "of the hundred new companies in this sector, only a few will reach viability." This will help you focus on separating winners from losers and choose the company with the best chances of survival. Instead of saying "this seems like an exciting opportunity," you should be saying "this is a game that's going to only have one or two winners—am I interviewing with one of these companies?"

4. Bet on management.

It's not a coincidence that the winners in the dot-com and PC booms were those companies led by seasoned management teams. If given the choice of going to work for a company with great technology and green management, and a company with mediocre technology and a seasoned group of pros at the controls, I'd choose the latter every time. It's no coincidence that bubble survivors Yahoo, Google, eBay, and Amazon are led by very experienced CEOs and vice presidents. When evaluating career opportunities, it's important to answer the question of "who's running the place?" Most reputable companies put executive bios on their websites under the "about us" link. You shouldn't expect to see an executive bio that says "I'm a total newbie." On the other hand, seeing that the person has had a successful track record makes the opportunity more interesting. The legal term "due diligence" describes the process of looking under the covers and seeing if the deal/company/person is really who it purports to be. Unfortunately, in the job realm, people aren't doing enough "due diligence."

Self Check-up

As you're thinking about the Top box of your life skills pyramid, you might consider asking yourself these questions:

1. What rewards "currency" are you playing for? Some of the more common forms are money, power, and self-satisfaction, although there are others. Before you wince at the word "power," it's only a bad word if it's used in a corruptible sense. Most of the hard-working elected officials are there trying to project the government's inherent powers for the greater good. It's okay to say you're in it for the money or conversely for the notion of helping the disadvantaged—the important thing is to know what you're playing for. In many cases, the flavors of possible rewards are mutually exclusive. For example, if you're in it for the psychographic benefit of feeling like you're making our schools a better place, you're probably also not going to make big money at the same time.

2. Do your rewards answer the question of what you want achieve while you're alive? You're going to spend 10,000 days pursuing this goal—is it worthy of that time investment? Ideally, we all should have an idea of the two or three things that we'd like to accomplish while we're on this planet. More than likely, one or more of these will come as a result of your life's work.

3. Are you thinking big enough? I spend a lot of time with entrepreneurs in my venture capital activities, and more often than not the person isn't thinking big enough. If you're like most high achievers, you're going to spend sixty hours per week (and most of your free thinking time outside of work) pursuing your goals. Whether they are big or small, it's probably going to consume your entire being for some number of years. Rather than spending your sixty hours opening up a health food store, why not advance your thinking to a nationwide chain or franchise concept? You could aspire to be a lawyer or to own your own law firm. Either choice is going to take 100 percent of your time and talents—so why not direct them to the higher upside opportunity?

Industry moguls like Donald Trump take this thinking to its farthest extreme. Often while they are in the process of executing their audacious plan to take over an industry, they'll run into a cash crunch. While the press headlines will be screaming that the project is about to fail, they seem serene and confident. What's the source of this confidence? They're worth more alive than dead. In other words, the bankers and investors who are financing the project will lose everything if it fails, but if they are patient, forgiving, and willing to put in a little more capital the project still has a chance of paying off. You might find it hard to line up a loan to purchase the house across the street from you, but find it relatively easy to put together an investor syndicate to reclaim a city block with a new housing concept.

With your Top box in place, we can now shift to the more tactical issues of building the skills you'll need to move across and up the levels in your pyramid. The next chapter deals with the essential workplace skills that trip up the majority of great people, for the most inexplicable reasons.

Over the next few weeks, make it a point to think about the Top box in your skills pyramid. If you think you already know where you are headed, then check yourself by filling out your pyramid outlining your plan for achieving your aspirations. If you're on track, this should be a simple and effortless process. Conversely, if you're not sure about what your Top box should say, then give yourself a decision deadline: *By this date, I am going to come to grips with my career goals.* Commit yourself to an introspective thought process designed to answer the question of what you want to do with your life. Talk to your friends in different industries, develop your own thesis for the future, read the business magazines. In short: take action. Tell yourself that each day you put this off you are consuming one of your precious 10,000 days.

Chapter 4

Master the Easy Stuff

There seems to be some perverse human characteristic
that likes to make easy things difficult.

—*Warren Buffett (b. 1930), American entrepreneur*

When you're a child, you tend to think of your family
home as a warm, protective, and often perfect shelter.
When you're the parent and homeowner, chances are that you
spend much more time thinking about the faults, flaws, and
needed repairs than the enjoyment the house brings you. A
manager looks at his business or team with the same critical
eye. While you might be a middle-of-the-bell-curve person
driving home thinking how much you enjoy working on this
team, at the same moment, in a different car, your manager is
probably obsessing about what to do with Frank, the weakest
member of the team; how poor Joe's presentation in the senior
management status meeting was; or worse, what he needs to do
to get *you* to move up or off the team. Same team, different
optics. For a manager, there's nothing more exasperating than

putting up with a glaring deficiency that should be a no-brainer, easy-to-fix issue for a person. In much the same way that you expect a certain level of courtesy when you check into a hotel or a gracious greeting at a fine restaurant, there's a certain level of capability that's expected of professional staff. So how often are managers exasperated or frustrated with employees who aren't able to do the easy things well? If you answered nearly every day, you're close. In truth, far more people have been held back, or put out to pasture, for consistently screwing up doing one of the easy things than people who have gotten ahead on pure intellect or exceptional skills. *That is, you're probably more likely to get promoted by just doing the easy things well than for your random exhibitions of brilliance.*

Great Expectations

I once had a woman who worked for me, who I'll call Ann, who was incredibly smart, driven, and committed to helping the company succeed. There was never a doubt that her heart and soul were poured into every assignment that made it on to her "to do" list. While Ann did many things exceptionally well, she had a chronic habit of showing up a few minutes late to nearly every meeting. When she would walk into my staff meetings late, I could sense that she had convinced herself that "I'm up to my ears with company-saving workload, so he's going to just have to be more understanding." Unfortunately, through my manager lens, I saw an out-of-control person, someone who was unable to appropriately manage her time in such a way that she could show the other eight people on my staff that she respected *their* time. More than once she embarrassed me by showing up for a customer meeting a few minutes late, and I could always count on her to be the last person to join an in-progress teleconference. She'd add stress to my business travel life, as I would sit there scanning the crowd of onboard passengers and not see her face. As the flight attendants made their last calls, I could only seethe about having to fly solo with a client without the appropriate presentation materials. Ann's deficiency started to become like that piece of parsley in your lunch date's teeth. Try as I might to focus my attention elsewhere, it was just too big of a distraction to ignore. While I'd try to rationalize this "minor" deficiency within the context of her overall contributions, in the end that voice in my head kept saying "she's out of control." Every time she would turn in a less than excellent performance, I just couldn't help attribute it to her inability to control her time. If a market analysis document had missing pieces, subconsciously I would be thinking, "She didn't allocate enough time to do a thorough job." I ended up firing Ann. A manager needs to have confidence in his people, and Ann had lost mine. Moral of the story: what's the difference between a person that looks completely out of control and someone who's not? About three minutes.

What could Ann have done to prevent or alter this career-limiting stigma? Simple. Shown up to meetings on time, every time. If that meant having to set her watch five minutes fast or getting to bed fifteen minutes earlier each evening, so be it. Keep in mind that no one on the team was getting checked off in an attendance book for being on-time. Of course not, because it's *expected* of a professional to be on time for a meeting. So, rather than being valued for her intellect and drive, Ann was committing career suicide because she wasn't exhibiting an expected skill. Unfortunately, the corporate wastelands are full of people who are being held back for the simplest reasons, ones that they just can't seem to grasp or address.

When you drop your car off to get fixed, you don't think to tell the mechanic not to get grease in your car's interior, because you *expect* this level of competence. Similarly, your company expects you to know enough to be punctual, write well, and dress appropriately. In many youthful company environments it's become normal for people to express and exhibit themselves in ways that would resulted in losing one's job a few years ago. If flip-flops or tie-dyed clothing are accepted at your workplace, make it the limit of your attention-getting efforts. While being perpetually late or sending off-color emails might make you a humorous favorite of your peers, it'll probably also ensure that you'll be there to entertain the next generation of peers with this unique but destructive talent. The manager's lens is a cruel judge that is programmed to filter out extraneous issues like how well liked you are by your peers.

Career-Stickers: The Easy Stuff That Trips People Up

So what are the easy things that trip otherwise good people up? They're the 101 workplace skills that we all know we should do well, but far too often neglect. When a manager is evaluating an employee for greater responsibility, she'll often put him in terms of "Can he do the easy things well?" The easy stuff comprises those things that you expect a twenty-something person to have mastered early in their career. I once had a boss who used to describe people as being "crisp," which meant the person was really on the ball. He would form his opinion based on how well the person did at executing the easy things.

It's a good idea to remember that your manager probably doesn't have the benefit of observing your every task and assignment. Instead, he probably gets random periods of time with you, given that he is managing six or ten others and he's got a boss of his own to be concerned about. A colleague of mine once joked that the definition of an executive is someone who can take a single point of data and extrapolate it to infinity. All joking aside, there's an element of truth here. Managers collect random bits of data on people and then extrapolate to form an overall image of the person. Right or wrong, it's the way it happens. He might see you in meetings, but more often he is going to see you in the way you handle accomplishing the easy things. As they say, perception is reality, and it's my belief that a big part of the perception equation for most people is how well they handle doing the easy things that are expected of them.

Take workplace dress as an example. Most high achievers either ignore casual Fridays or simply dial the formalness level down from wool slacks to khakis or a woman's business suit to comfortable slacks and a sweater. I've yet to see a company name casual Friday "Self-Expression Day," although you can almost always count on the attention-starved to show up in their faded jeans, tank tops, or half-shirts. These people might be thinking: "Hank, the chief scientist, comes in a Hawaiian shirt, shorts, and sandals, so let the dress-down party begin." Through my manager's lens, I am more than likely thinking: "Hank has thirty-four patents to his name, and if he wants to wear a Speedo to work he's earned that right. Sally, on the other hand, whom I'm trying to decide whether or not she's on the management track, doesn't give off grown-up, ready-to-manage vibes with her flip-flops and half-shirt." A good, safe rule of thumb for the workplace is to be slightly overdressed instead of flirting with the bounds of decency. Sounds simple, but you'll never go wrong being overdressed.

Being punctual and dressing appropriately are two of the essential do-the-easy-stuff-well skills that a young professional must possess. Here's a list of seemingly no-brainers that need to be adapted as personal law in the workforce if you are to achieve great things with your career:

Promptly Returning Phone Calls and Email Correspondence

Most people procrastinate when it comes to returning phone calls and emails. Given the high volume of corporate communications today, it's no wonder there are times when we just want to ignore the whole issue. Of course, the situation is exacerbated if the call involves a difficult person or a troubled situation. The conflict avoidance center in our brains is constantly saying *tomorrow*. The truth is, this correspondence needs to be promptly addressed. The best approach is to make your rule to never leave the office without having closed these open doors. A solid piece of advice would be to handle items needing a reply as a first priority, whatever the situation. If you were to express this issue as a mathematical equation, it would look something like: *The Problem x Festering Time = Severity of the Crisis.* Most customers, colleagues, clients, and bosses are reasonable people when you're promptly communicating the actions you are taking to resolve their issue. On the other hand, with sufficient time to fester, the smallest problems can become a serious mark on an otherwise unblemished track record. I'd prefer an employee give me regular updates that say "I don't yet have an answer, but here's what I'm doing to get one," than to have that feeling of slowly rising blood pressure that's part of feeling that a problem is in a black hole.

Saying Thank You

Over the years, I have given countless wedding gifts to employees, sent flowers to the memorial services for someone close to a colleague, and have contributed my personal funds to a staff member's favorite charity and, I'm sorry to say, it was the minority of people who sent a thank you note for these gestures of support. Now don't get me wrong—this wouldn't cause me to sulk about not being appreciated. Instead, it makes me think: "Harry seems to be lacking in the social graces area. I probably couldn't trust him in a customer facing position where these skills are required." If you're thinking "that's so passé," your manager might be thinking you lack the minimum social graces that are required of senior managers in their dealings with customers, employees, and vendors. The moral of the story: go on the Internet and order a set of pre-printed note cards (with your professional name on the top) and be prepared to use them. This $50 investment will go a long way towards demonstrating that you are a mature, gracious, and thoughtful person.

Dressing Well

The way we dress has a big impact on how we are perceived by our bosses, colleagues, and customers. Take a look around and I'll bet you'll see there's a noticeable correlation between your company's executive talent and dressing well. Our clothes can radiate competence, impeccable taste, total ignorance, or a complete lack of professionalism. We all have moments of crisis in the closet, wondering whether this jacket, tie, or dress will work in the office—although these aren't the truly serious matters. The bigger issues are the ruts that we fall into, resulting in us being unable to see ourselves the way others perceive us. In essence, we think that traditional blue suit, white shirt, and red tie looks so "classic," when our observers are thinking, "He looks like a 70s caricature of the IBM guy." This "can't see it" phenomenon isn't too different from avocado green plaid curtains in your parents' house—they just don't see them anymore. It's important to realize that dressing well is something that we all have to work at; including devoting a few hours per month of time to looking our best.

I once knew a guy who had great aspirations and excellent potential but was a horrible dresser. While he thought he knew his way around a men's store, the reality was that he was like so many males—he wasn't seeing a clear picture in the mirror. The term "dress for success" has a ring of truth to it. If you look around you, you'll see that the majority of the senior executives that you know are well-dressed people. This gentleman was "saved" by a talented, forceful department salesman who saw a guy with promise who just didn't know how to dress the part. How do I know so much about this person? I sheepishly admit this person was me.

So what can you do to nail this easy thing and appear competent in this important area? Here's some gender specific guidance:

The well-dressed man...

• Never makes someone uncomfortable with his dress. If his client's office is casual dress, he doesn't show up in a suit. If it's a dark suit and tie environment, he doesn't show up in a tweed jacket.

• Realizes that cotton pants have no place in the office. Ever. Cheap $35 cotton khakis wrinkle and bunch up, particularly when sitting at a desk all day, turning the most sophisticated guy into a wrinkled fraternity brother again. Wool is your friend, gents—winter weight in the fall and winter, tropical weight in the spring and summer. Trust me, your boss's boss wishes you would understand this.

• Won't wear pastel anything. No pink oxford shirts, no yellow sweaters, no light green ties. It's so college.

• Never wears a promotional logo on his shirt or jacket unless it's a paid sponsorship. You're not a NASCAR driver. What do you do with the T-shirts and golf shirts vendors give you? Anything but wear them in public. This "look" screams "I'm so cheap and unsophisticated that I'll even wear a shirt that makes me an advertising shill for this computer company."

• Knows that the little gold buttons on an inexpensive blue blazer is a country club look—not for the office. If you've got one of these, do yourself a favor and invest the $20 to have a tailor to replace them with the dark blue variety.

• Spends 20 percent of his clothes budget on accessories. Watch her eyes, and the first place they go is to your watch. A cheap plastic watch says "he's a cheapskate," and the $79 pair of dress shoes says "unsophisticated." The wrong belt with the right slacks ruins the look. Most guys think people don't spend much time looking beyond their pants and shirt, which couldn't be further from the truth. Shoes, belts, and watches make or break the outfit. Incidentally, wing-tips haven't been in since the 70s. It's the details that bring the look together.

• Aims to match harmonious colors versus contrasting colors. There's a flaw in the male mind that makes us want to match a yellow shirt with brown pants, a red shirt with black pants, or a blue shirt with crème-colored khakis. The better approach is a single palette, like a gray shirt with gray slacks or a blue shirt with blue trousers. Clothing designers talk about "the silhouette" to describe the way clothes look as they drape your body. A single color palette is their oldest and most reliable trick in the book.

- Doesn't wear cologne, bracelets, or a ring other than one that signifies marriage.

- Has a card in his wallet of the name of his regular salesman at Nordstrom or Bloomingdales. He's got a relationship with this guy during which they get together a few times each year to tune up his wardrobe. If this doesn't sound very macho, I must inform you that your company's executive team is a little less macho than you think. You really can't do this by yourself; you need someone to nudge you in a direction away from yesterday's plaid shirts, overly pleated pants, or wing-tip shoes, otherwise you end up in a rut you can't see.

The well-dressed woman...

- Knows that the male mind is hopelessly one-track. Femininity in the workplace is okay, sexy is not.

- Is confident enough in her abilities that she doesn't feel the need to dress like a man. Appropriately conservative and feminine attire says "Yes, I'm a woman, but don't take me lightly."

- Realizes that women get lumped into two groups: the well-dressed professional look and the young unsophisticated girl. You can't go back and forth between the two successfully.

- Has a business casual repertoire that doesn't include anything faded, stretched, or studded.

- Never wears jewelry on her lapel, including bumblebees, lady bugs, flowers, or flags.

- Never grooms herself in public. Ever.

- Creates lasting memories with her intellectual capacity and not the breadth of her closet. If a guy wears a bright orange shirt, it's forgotten within hours. If a woman wears a hot pink dress, people will be able to recall the image for months.

- Never wears flip flops, sandals, faded jeans, beads of any kind, or leggings to work.

- Knows that details matters. Swatch watches are cute, but they don't go with a business outfit. Too much makeup is distracting, and too little says "I just rolled out of bed."

Expense Reporting

Someone could probably write an entire book on the subject of stupid employee expense account tricks. It may include a story about a senior manager with whom I worked who tried to submit all of the prior year's expenses in the first month of a new fiscal year; the $2,000 bar tab that was disguised as a meeting, and the creative guy who always seemed to have lunches that came in round numbers like $30, $40, or $60. Here's an easy set of rules to follow:

- **Always submit your expense reports within two weeks of incurring the expenses.** If you're on a trip, why not fill out the expense report on the airplane or train ride home? Why does timeliness matter? Well, if your manager sends you to an expensive conference in June, she's probably thinking that this will hit her budget in July when your expense report arrives. If, on the other hand, you submit your expense report in November, and that's already a tight budget month for her, you might be the reason she's blown her expense budget in front of *her* boss. Nearly every manager has to show competence in handling a budget. Handling expense reports is a mini-version of demonstrating this competency. Will it get you promoted if you nail every expense report with perfection and submit them in a timely manner? Perhaps not—but being sloppy in this area could be a like an anchor around your neck.

- **If you're ever unsure about an expense, either delete it or ask for advice from your boss.** You never want him thinking "What the heck is this?" when he's reading your expense report. And, if you're really good, you'll get pre-approval for those items that are sure to catch someone's attention. If the only hotel you can find is a five-star, you mention to your boss ahead of time that the city is booked and that you might not have a choice but to stay in an expensive hotel. Similarly, seeking his advice about taking the client team out to a fine French restaurant ahead of time is good form if this isn't the norm.

- **Don't make the mistake of observing others as a method for setting your expense standards.** It will almost always lead to trouble. Most companies publish their expense standards; it's easy enough to read these and adhere to the letter of the law. Just because "everybody" stays at the Hyatt, it isn't a good reason for you to violate the corporate expense rules. The person in the accounting office who is responsible for expense reports almost always has a keen eye and a penchant to whisper to managers about their people.

• **Never cheat—it's just not worth it.** Getting away with a few hundred dollars of expense report inflation could cost you your integrity, or your job, which is a poor trade for most all professionals.

Understanding the Mission and Structure of the Organization

There's nothing like sitting with a young person and realizing the person doesn't have a clue about what's going on around him. He doesn't know the company's mission, organization structure, or priorities. Through the manager's lens, this lack of knowledge will nearly always come off as a self-absorbed person who couldn't give a damn what happens outside of his cubicle. You owe it to your company to understand the basics of the mission, strategy, and organization. If you work for a public company, this information is disclosed in the form of public filings. It's inexcusable if you're not reading these disclosures. Sites like Yahoo Finance make it easy to access this information. If your company is private, it simply means that you have to listen harder and ask more questions.

Knowing the Art of Making Introductions

Knowing how to introduce people is becoming a dying art. The cop-out method of today is to ask everyone in the meeting to go around the table and introduce themselves. If you want to look crisp, you'll know how to make an appropriate introduction. A good introduction includes not only the person's name but a few sentences that will link the person to the other party or to the situation at-hand. So, rather than introducing your boss to your customer by saying, "This is John," you would say, "Mark, I'd like you to meet John Taylor, who heads up procurement for Mega Corp. You and John have something in common: he, too, loves to fly fish." As the person receiving the introduction, this exchange automatically puts me at ease, because we've got something to talk about from the onset of our meeting. And if you're really good at this skill, you'll be viewed as a gracious and skilled host when you work the crowd to introduce people that either have similar interests or are looking uncomfortable because they don't know anyone. Taking Rich by the arm to meet Caroline and saying, "Caroline, I'd like you to meet Rich Smith, who heads up the creative team at XYZ Corp. You're always receiving his invoices, and I thought it might be nice to place a face with an invoice" will earn you points all the way around.

Avoiding Surprises

When I reflect on all of the "A" players who have worked for me, I can consistently say that the best of the best never turn up unwanted surprises. If they're going to come up short on a scheduled delivery or a financial expectation, they let you know far in advance the progress they are making towards their deliverables. It's the "B" player who informs you the day of the meeting, in the middle of the crisis, or at the end of the quarter that there's a big problem that can't be solved quickly. The problem with surprises is that they almost always require a reporting of a surprise further up the line, and you've just put the manager in the position of having to surprise his boss, which your manager is not supposed to do at this level in his career.

Seizing the Initiative

Many are the employees who do exactly what they are told and nothing more. Few are the stars who take the initiative without needing to hear a directive. Your manager should be thinking of you with the blissful thought that you're out there exhibiting good judgment and adding to your "to do" list with the best interest of the department and the company in mind. He needs to know that he can count on you to recognize an unanswered problem and take the initiative to solve it.

Are you about to let down an important client? Please don't wait for your manager to ask whether you've talked to the customer and walked him through the problem. If your team is about to miss an important date, you should be ready to discuss a three-point plan your company will need to execute a remediation effort. The CEO of a company is used to managing a team of self-starters who need very little supervision to accomplish there objectives. It's a beautiful thing to supervise a team like this—people who take the initiative and back it with great execution. You can give your boss a taste of this feeling by giving him the implicit sense that you're his go-to person, the one who's always one step ahead of the situation. You'll also have a key ally when it comes time to nominate someone for a promotion.

You May Be Failing When It Comes to the Easy Stuff

Sometimes I wonder if some people have a self-destruct gene that is programmed to exhibit a career-limiting behavior. There are countless very competent first-level employees with desks, cubes, or offices that are a wreck. This person may think it makes him an interesting character. Does he really think his manager will consider him for promotion when he looks this out of control? His manager is not likely to risk letting him set this standard of disorganization for a team of valued people. He may not be fired over it, but he's probably also not going to be sponsored for a promotion.

Take the guy who doesn't take the time to capitalize, use appropriate salutations, punctuate, or spell-check his emails. Doesn't he realize that emails might be forwarded beyond his intended target? Being seen as a character among his peers might be desirable for him, although when the manager's lens comes into focus it's rarely a good thing to be seen as "colorful."

Keep in mind, people don't get fired for not doing one or more of the easy things well. It's actually more insidious than that. They typically find themselves being passed over and typecast at a level they don't think they deserve. There are a lot of poorly dressed middle-career people with bad work habits that sit around whining that the world isn't fair. Not doing the easy stuff well is like showing up to the race with a nonconforming car. Your advancement hopes might be doomed before you reach the starting gate.

Can you overcome a big "easy thing" deficiency through sheer brilliance? Sure, but why would you try? Wouldn't it just be easier to set your watch five minutes faster and save your tie-dye for the weekends? We can find exceptions to nearly every rule, although for my money and career, I prefer to stick to playing the percentages. The objective is to showcase your talents, with the minimum amount of distraction. A manager expects a young person to have a few rough edges, and he expects she just needs time to hone them down. But, when a crisp young person bursts onto the scene, age ceases to be a consideration. The competence she exudes says, "Give the ball to me; I can handle it," and she soon finds herself on a faster track.

Chapter 5

The Art of Being Coachable

All of us, at certain moments of our lives,
need to take advice and to receive help from other people.

—*Alexis Carrel (1873-1944), French surgeon,
sociologist, biologist, and Noble Prize winner*

I marvel at the abilities of the players when I watch sports, but what impresses me the most is not necessarily their outstanding athleticism. When a quarterback trots off the field after throwing a key interception or a soccer goalie misses a crucial shot, he is often greeted by his coach with a vocal chewing out. While most spectators probably see a chastened player, I see someone with an incredibly high tolerance for feedback. How many of us could stay focused on the game after being booed off the field and screamed at by our boss in front of thousands of people? Often the coach's tirade includes a few improvement points, and more often than not, the player responds with a victorious contribution later in the game.

Much like an athlete, professionals need to develop resilience, tolerance, and a desire for criticism. *The art of being coachable is being open to the feedback of others, and most importantly, possessing a willingness to act upon this feedback.* A large part of progressing towards your career objective involves knowing when you're falling short. Often it will be your manager or supervisor who is best able to see the areas in which you need improvement. But the coaching process is frequently broken or nonexistent. If an employee's implicit goal is to get ahead in life and a manger's explicit role is to help the employee achieve her goals (for the benefits of both the employee and the company), how can it be that the coaching process is so damaged? Isn't this practice the essence of the employee/manager relationship?

It is certainly logical to think that the manager and employee relationship would be centered on coaching. But in the real world, it is often a dysfunctional relationship. The vast majority of people in the workforce are not coachable, which is unfortunate because it's probably the lynchpin issue that's holding them back from achieving their goals. These employees are more comfortable with the status quo, and more content to mire in the dead-end muck than face the hard work associated with personal growth. Or they are afraid to admit their weaknesses, thus appearing not good enough for the job.

The most successful career achievers all possess three important traits directly related to coaching: courage to change, honesty in goal-setting, and a high acceptance of criticism. In this chapter, we will look at how to foster these attributes and why they are essential to your career. We'll also address how you can assist your manager in giving you helpful instruction and steps you need to implement for improvement.

If this is starting to sound like hard work…you're right. As with most things in the workplace, if it was easy, it would pay minimum wage.

Here's a lesson from early in my career. Three years out of college, I was up for a promotion as manager of a ten-person group. Hewlett-Packard's policy was to hold a formal interview process among the

> "If people knew how hard I worked to get my mastery, it wouldn't seem so wonderful after all."
>
> —*Michelangelo*

available internal candidates. I was sure I was the best person for the job: I had the best track record, a great relationship with my higher-ups—I thought my career was on a roll. Of course, all this added to my shock and embarrassment when the promotion was awarded to one of my competitors. A few days into my stewing and disappointment, I was approached by the senior manager who had made the decision. He asked me if I'd like to know why I didn't get the position. Thinking he was going to buck me up, I was surprised when he did the opposite. He gave me some of the most brutal feedback I had heard in my young life. We talked about several of my deficiencies. Specifically, he suggested I work on how I presented myself and focus on the perceptions that I was leaving with others. His words still stick with me today: "You aren't well self-actualized." What he meant was that I didn't understand how I was coming across to people in my business interactions. To say I was bowled over is putting it mildly. As I picked myself up off the proverbial floor and dusted myself off, I somehow found the ability to resist giving a "yeah, but" response, thanked him for his feedback, and left to go home.

For the first part of the drive I was mad at him and later at myself for letting things get this far off-track. But over the next few days his feedback had a chance to sink in, and I realized that not only was he right, but everything he was saying was completely in my control. It wasn't like he was saying I was too short or had the wrong eye color; rather, he was telling me exactly what I needed to do to get the job the next time. His feedback was cathartic; all I had to do was digest what he had to say, put a plan in place to make the necessary corrections, then execute the plan. Not only did I get the job the next time around, but I was a better person and better prepared for having been through this feedback loop.

Possess the Courage to Change

Personal growth involves sticking your neck out and saying, "I'm not good at this, and I need to be better." It takes a lot of courage to achieve your personal objectives. Growing can often be a frightening process because step one involves your admission that you have a deficiency. Our subconscious minds, which often act as control centrals for our fears and insecurities, are very effective at steering us away from openly recognizing—and admitting—our own shortcomings.

Change-related fear often manifests itself as being afraid of the "trappings" of success. You may fear that as you grow, so too will the expectations people hold for you. We often see this phenomenon in children. The child quickly learns that learning to tie one's own shoes comes with a new expectation that she can now dress herself. It's little wonder why childhood growth spurts are often followed by periods of regression.

Unfortunately, many people with great potential lack the necessary courage to grow and develop. Dare to change, and the payoff will come.

Accept—and Encourage—Criticism

High achievers thrive on real-time feedback. They have a constant thirst for self-improvement criticism, and they lean heavily on their bosses to provide it. They know that "winning" means attaining their goals, not prevailing in their arguments with the bosses. They are a joy to manage—with the only downside being they get promoted out from under you fairly quickly.

But for every employee who allows himself to benefit from the coaching process, there are far more who reject it. They let that natural fight or flight instinct take over. Without even realizing it, they're putting up walls between themselves and the one person who is best positioned to help them achieve their goals.

On my way to becoming a better manager, I learned an important point about coaching. After a meeting in which my team presented our ideas for a new product concept, my boss asked me to stay behind for a brief discussion. He said, "You did a really effective job of defending your team and getting *your* point across. The problem is, when you're doing that, you're no longer a member of the senior management team. Instead you're just one of the people on the team we can critique." In other words, he was telling me that when I assumed that defensive feedback repelling crouch, I was so focused my defense that I wasn't learning and absorbing. If you ever wonder why the best managers normally have their people doing all the presenting, you now have the answer. We've all heard the old adage that says you aren't learning when you're mouth is open. Let's add another one: you're not learning when you're defending yourself.

Accepting Criticism

For the sake of the following discussion, let's assume that you have a good manager who wants to be proactive in helping you be a better employee. Later in this chapter we'll address what you need to do if you have a manager who isn't this focused on helping you grow and learn in your position.

Here's an example from an earlier period of my career that illustrates how crucial learning from feedback is. Bill worked for me as a salesman of expensive high-tech equipment. While others achieved higher sales levels or had up-and-down streaks, Bill was a solid guy who always made his numbers and was well-liked by his customers and peers. I thought I saw something in Bill that others didn't see—that he could be a great salesman, with a little coaching. Together we constructed a personal development plan focusing on what I believed were the key skill areas in which he could and should grow. We agreed to review his progress in frank discussions at least once a month.

In our first meeting I planned to review Bill's progress against his three important improvement areas, the first of which was his sales closing technique. (In the sales profession there's probably no skill more important than the ability to ask for the order. Do it too soon and you're considered pushy and obnoxious. Do it too late and you've wasted you and your company's time.) I mentioned to Bill that he seemed uncertain and reluctant to ask for the customer's business and that he would probably see both his sales numbers and the size of his commission checks increase with improved technique in this area.

Sadly, what came next started a long and frustrating pattern in our discussions, which to my knowledge, are still repeating fifteen years later. Bill is still "back there" while many of his peers have gone on to bigger, better, and more interesting things. He was the master of a destructive communication style that I call *point-counterpoint*, a common behavior that acts like arsenic in the coaching well.

Here's how it went. I said something like: "Bill, when we were out at Clark Company, I was reading all the signs that the customer was ready to buy our system. Rather than go for the close, you offered to do another demonstration. By doing so, you ended up giving our competition more time to mount a comeback and unnecessarily lengthened the sales cycle." Bill replied, "Rob, I don't think you saw me at my best. When I'm by myself on a sales call I'm typically more aggressive and always asking for the business." When I told him that I observed this skill weakness in other situations, he replied that I was being unfair to him and that I wasn't seeing "the real Bill."

Point-counterpoint. I made a suggestion, Bill responded with a counterpoint that offered nothing to the equation other than putting a cap on the learning process.

You may be asking yourself: "Don't managers ever make bad calls? Shouldn't I point something out if I believe he's wrong? After all, this is my career swinging in the balance!" In a word: No.

Companies and organizations rely and depend on hierarchy. A recipe for anarchy would be a system that encouraged employees to constantly question the judgments of their managers. In practice, the manager is well-positioned to observe and measure the employee. They work in the same office, attend many of the same meetings, and they interact on a daily basis—like the umpire in baseball, their position is conceived to give them a good vantage point. Accept his feedback, even if you feel that one or two points might be off-base. This acceptance is much smarter than risking your "coachability" playing point-counterpoint. Here's the upshot: if you are clear about your willingness to be coached, your manager will want to spend more time with you. It only takes one or two occurrences for a manager to conclude you aren't coachable—or worthy of the efforts he would make to help you improve your job.

If you play point-counterpoint, your manager may come to the conclusion that you aren't willing to grow, and decide that his time is better spent working with a different employee. It's natural for your manager to want to spend time with people who are eager to learn and grow. It's refreshing and incredibly rewarding to feel like you are helping someone. Great managers live for this. Conversely, trying to coach someone who has stopped learning is as much fun as skiing uphill. Are there lots of Bills out there? More than you might think. In fact, Bill's point-counterpoint behavior pattern is more the norm than the exception.

Encouraging Criticism

"A" players are proactive in seeking out constructive criticism. They thrive on hearing any and all feedback in an effort to improve themselves. If the "B" player is the hyper-sensitive opera diva who's in danger of cracking at the hint of anything less than exultation, the "A" team is made up of self-assured people who are saying, "bring it on, let me have it." Their best-case scenario is to have a boss that feeds them a constant stream of constructive but honest feedback. The less than ideal scenario is when they have the more typical species of boss, who doesn't provide direct feedback out of a fear of conflict. They have managers who will help them address their shortcomings and work towards improving them. In the worst-case scenarios, they are not able to help you progress in your work and you're not ever going to grow and learn under them.

Here's a story that demonstrates the importance of encouraging critical feedback and instruction. Jane is someone I worked with early in my career. To this day, she is one of the fastest rising stars in her industry, and she is always a favorite with the executives with whom she works. The secret to her success isn't that she's smarter, more politically adept, or the product of an ivy university—it's that she's more coachable than her peers. She's willing to seek constructive criticism, listen to it, learn from it, and then take meaningful action.

During a semi-annual performance review, one of the company's newest managers started the meeting by extolling

Jane's virtues in the typical high-fluff/no-substance tradition of employee reviews. Jane let the performance review unfold for about five minutes until she politely interjected with, "It's really great to hear how well I am doing, and I am glad I am meeting or exceeding your expectations in many areas of my job. But frankly, I already know where I'm strong. What I really want to hear about are the areas where I am in the greatest need of growth. I recognize that I don't know everything there is to know about this job; I need you to tell me the three or four areas where I'm in the most need of improvement. You already know about my desire to become a sales V.P., so feel free to tie these feedback points to prep areas for my next position on the way to achieving my goal. I'm hoping you'll give me some personal instruction as well as recommendations for any seminars, books, or role models within the company that will help me with these deficiencies. Perhaps we should review my progress every month or so, and once we knock off this list we can start another."

There is nothing more enjoyable for a manager than to lead someone who is open to the learning process. Most people are growth-adverse, which often makes supervisory positions so stressful and thankless. Jane's commitment to personal growth was both refreshing and demanding for her manager. In one respect, his job becomes easier because he doesn't have to deal with the typical barriers to learning and growth. On the other hand, Jane has succeeded in making his job more demanding—and rewarding. He now must now be a collaborator in her career progression. In essence, she has co-opted him for her personal gain. In the end, it's truly a win-win situation.

If you have a strong manager you might feel like you are getting what you need from your relationship with your boss. If, on the other hand, you're like most people who have a manager who gets a "C" grade in coaching, then it's important for you to take the lead. What are the ingredients of a successful coaching relationship between a manager and an employee? The recipe looks as follows:

1. There's a shared personal development between you and your manager. This plan should highlight the three or four skills area where you need the most help.

2. You create an environment where your manager is free to give you direct criticism.

3. You have an agreement to meet regularly to review your progress on the plan.

Be Honest in Setting Your Goals

As you engage your boss in the goal-setting process, be truthful with yourself. Unfortunately, most people who state that they want to grow, develop, and be promoted aren't honest with themselves about what they want. In this sense, the coaching process can be a lot of talk, with little true intent to back up those words.

The person who is genuinely interested in being coached to higher levels of performance has already contemplated the costs and benefits of opening this door. If he's aiming for a supervisory role, he's already contemplated the good and bad that goes along with managing people. If he desires securing an overseas assignment, he has been taking language lessons for the past few years. Often the less-than-sincere pretender comes forward after a life-changing event, which could come in the form of financial stresses at home or the promotion of a best friend. He is interested in attaining the benefits of advancement without giving adequate thought to the "costs" involved.

Here are some questions to ask yourself to test if you are honest in your goals:

- What is my ultimate career goal?
- Why do I *really* want this position?
- What are the positives of achieving this goal?
- What are some of the drawbacks?
- What am I willing to do to achieve this goal?

Let me tell you about a woman who worked for me as a technical support person, visiting customers to help them better use our products. Sally was sharp, coachable, committed, and praised by customers. One day she approached me about her new goal—to be a salesperson. In a very short amount of time, she went from being an excellent technical person to a failing salesperson. Try as I might, it just seemed that everything I did to help her made the situation more miserable. Sally failed as a salesperson, and I failed her as her coach.

What I neglected to do was probe the sincerity of Sally's desire to become a sales pro and to have her explore her own reasons for wanting this career change. Had I taken the time to do so, I would have seen that Sally lacked the underlying desire to take on this new career challenge. She was a very young professional, just a few years out of college. She looked at the salesperson's role as a glamorous profession. The job description would read like one of those ads in the back of a magazine: *Earn $200,000 per year, be your own boss, make your own hours.* In Sally's case, she learned very quickly that for every exhilarating moment, there are hours of frustration, rejection, and self-doubt that go along with the sales profession.

My enthusiasm for taking on a new coaching assignment ultimately served to do Sally a grave disservice and teach me a valuable lesson about coaching people. It is crucial to be honest with yourself as you engage your boss in the goal-setting process. Your boss wants to see that you are honest in your commitment to devote your entire self, without reservation, to this objective. Let's say your stated goal is be the manager of your present customer support department. Okay, that's great, but you need to convince both your boss *and* yourself that you are truly interested in making the commitment to exceed in this new endeavor. Sure, the desired job might get a bigger cube, more money, and more prestige, but it might also come with a new set of demands associated with added responsibility.

Let's go back to our honesty checklist and break down "What are some of the drawbacks" of being the manager of the customer support department:

- Are you ready to fire people?
- Are you ready to hire people and have your performance judged by the quality of your hires?
- Are you ready to sit down and have frank coaching sessions with poor performers?

If you answered no to the above questions, you'd soon find yourself viewed as a weak manager, surrounded by poor performers who don't seem to be getting better. If you aren't happy in your present position, take a moment to imagine what it would be like to live in this newly created pressure cooker.

People often come to me to talk about their desire to pursue a promotion or new position, but they lack the commitment to do what it will take to accomplish this goal. In an interview situation, this lack of desire is easily uncovered and often results in a no-hire outcome. If the person does slip through the cracks and gets the job, it's difficult, if not impossible, to coach him towards these objectives, because the employee's lack of authenticity will ultimately manifest itself in a lack of follow-through and commitment.

There's a key point to keep in mind as you assess the level of honesty that underlies your goals. Goal-setting, by definition, means stretching yourself beyond where you already are. I've never met a manager who wasn't scared to death to take that first supervisory role or a new project manager who wasn't trembling when he realized it was now his neck firmly in the noose. The point isn't to make you reluctant to stretch yourself and take on increasingly more responsibility but instead to encourage you to take in the whole picture prior to announcing your candidacy. This deliberate examination will allow you to weigh the implications of your actions and help you identify the developmental steps you'll need to take to succeed in this endeavor.

Help Your Manager Help You

At the top of every leader's objectives list should be the growth and development of his or her people. Sadly, this is where many leaders fail to shine. Therefore, to be really successful as a career professional, you need to learn to lead your boss. When Jane took things into her own hands, she added symmetry to the manager/employee coaching relationship. Both parties have an important role to play. Jane's approach forces the manager to be a thoughtful coach for their mutual gains. If her approach serves as a forcing function to make the manager a better coach, hallelujah! While her peers are sitting through fluff reviews and playing point-counterpoint, Jane is getting actionable coaching that corresponds with her stated career goals.

Let's suppose you were a skier with great potential but you were unable to break into the list of Olympic medal contenders. Let's also say that you possessed the attitude of the Typical Employee. There you are, slope-side with your coach, only wanting to hear the positive and painless commentary on how great your last downhill run was. Your coach suffers from Typical Manager Disease. He plays along and feeds you lots of fluff and very little instruction that is actionable to improve your performance. Think you'll make it to the top with this approach? Of course you won't. If you want to be the best, you're going to have to insist that your coach or boss points out every weakness in technique, attitude, and ability that he believes impedes your success. If you're smart, you'll wring out every bit of advice that he has to offer—and begin to implement the changes he suggests.

In the real world of the workplace, people don't live up to their full potential for very real reasons. Our protective subconscious mind wants us to believe that there is a mysterious and unfair force that holds people back and propels others ahead. In reality, it's usually as simple as two managers getting together and discussing an employee's progress. When your boss's boss asks your boss "How is Fred doing?" or "Should we consider him for promotion this year?" your manager is almost certainly going to talk about your strengths and weaknesses. Perhaps he'll say, "Fred excels at customer communications but needs more work on X, Y, and Z. I don't think he's ready yet." Wouldn't you rather your manager be able to say, "Fred excels at customer communications and has improved his progress on X, Y, and Z. Fred and I discussed these areas during last year's performance review, and I'm pleased that he has worked hard to improve himself in these areas since that discussion. He's ready for the additional responsibility this promotion would entail."

Maintain a Rational Definition of Winning

The coaching process isn't about being right or wrong—it's about lessons and learning. *Winning in the career game means accomplishing your goals, achieving your financial aspirations, and making a contribution to your employer's business.* Nowhere in that definition will you find "being right" or "protecting one's ego from bruises." None of us have all the answers, but if you come home from work feeling like you've grown, it can be considered a good day.

In more than twenty years of coaching high-achievers, I've never seen a born leader, "a natural", or a gifted employee. Every career achiever I know became successful through hard work and commitment. I'm not talking about fourteen-hour work days, although there is some degree of correlation between long hours and career achievement. I'm talking about mastering the art of being coachable—being open to the feedback of others and possessing a willingness to act upon this feedback—that will aid you in developing and implementing your personal growth objectives. Commit yourself to encouraging and accepting criticism as well as putting suggestions into action, and you'll find yourself a high-achiever in your career.

Chapter 6

An Action-Oriented Curiosity

Curiosity is one of the permanent and certain characteristics
of a vigorous mind.

—*Samuel Johnson (1709-1784), British man of letters*

We're all familiar with the idiomatic phrase "curiosity
killed the cat." For my payroll dollars, this adage
couldn't be further from the truth. An active curiosity, coupled
with a willingness to act on it, makes someone incredibly
valuable. The average employee is far too eager to let the
unexplained remain a mystery, while the "A" player isn't
satisfied until he truly understands what makes his world tick.
He realizes that knowledge is power *and* it has to be acquired.

So if information equals power, what can you do to get
more of it? Most "A" players have developed a set of
techniques and habits that allows them to harness the information sources at their disposal. In this chapter, we'll discuss
the avenues you can take to acquire—and use—this
information.

How do you recognize if it's a lack of curiosity that's holding somebody back? You'll find it in otherwise bright people who have a blind spot when it comes to understanding financial accounting concepts, in a sales representative who only has a superficial knowledge of a product, or in the customer service person who doesn't understand the underlying science that makes the product work. Through the manager's optics, these deficiencies come off as laziness, or worse, a lack of commitment to the company. Most managers are selected from the ranks of high achievers, so they've come to expect the same standard of commitment they ask of themselves in their employees. It drives them nuts when an otherwise bright person refuses to engage his brain.

Here's a situation that happens almost daily in companies. A meeting takes place during which the president or general manager reviews the progress of the organization. During his presentation, he might mention the importance of attaining Six Sigma quality in a particular area or ISO 9001 certification. His talk might discuss financial performance measures, like operating profits, EBITA, and cost of goods sold. During the question and answer session, someone queries him on the reasons for the recent volatility in the company's stock price, and he talks about Wall Street's expectations and how the company's earnings per share were impacted by special charges. As the manager is presenting his information, most of the people allow themselves to glaze over at these foreign concepts. They think: "All this accounting mumbo jumbo is so complicated—thank God we have those bean counters to understand it all." And that's where they leave it.

Now, somewhere in the back of the room there's an "A" player with an active curiosity. As the manager is presenting, she makes a note in the margins of her paper: *Six Sigma, Operating Profit Calculations, and Special Charges.* When she returns to her desk, she writes these three things on her "to do" list, which might lead her to "Google" for an answer, order a book, or ask a few questions of her friend in Accounting. As you can see, rather than taking the path of least resistance, she's actively engaging her curiosity. In the same way that learning a foreign language expands the processing capability of your brain, developing your intellectual curiosity will make a huge contribution to your professional development. When I solicit answers from my staff members, I can always tell when I'm hearing from someone with a well-developed curiosity. The answers reflect a great deal of introspection—typically they've already been pondering a problem long before my interrogation.

I once worked for a great manager who taught me something about applying curiosity to a problem. I had a problem employee who was a drag on my team and our results were suffering. He was a bright young product manager who couldn't get along with the research and development team. This friction was causing our product timelines to slip and requiring me to spend more time refereeing and less time on customer-focused activities. I was ready to cut bait on the guy and told my manager in a one-on-one that I was commencing a process to exit this employee from the company. My manager's reaction was elucidating. He said, "Rob, when we hired Jim we were sure he was going to be a killer hire for your team. He had the right résumé of experiences and skills, and he came with great references. Very few people come to work every day saying, 'Today's the day I'm really going to suck at my job.' So let's assume for a second that Jim isn't in this minority and that he really wants to succeed in his career. What is it about our culture that takes a great guy like Jim and turns him into a poor performer?" Talk about turning a problem inside out; I hadn't taken the time to look at the problem from this perspective. My boss's curiosity wouldn't let him see the problem from only one side of the prism. He couldn't help but take the problem, spin it around, and look at it from every angle. As it turns out, Jim worked out to be a good employee. It seems that a few managers in other departments had been taking advantage of Jim's newness, thus, not giving him the information and face time to get his job done.

Brain Food

Top performers are always well-informed. These people are information sponges about their company, their products, their industry, and their world. They're voracious readers, Web surfers, listeners, and observers. Additionally, their information stores extend to their knowledge about people, including themselves. So if information equals power, what can you do to get more of it? "A" players have developed a set of techniques and habits that allows them to harness the information sources at their disposal. You need to develop these as well.

Much like the grazing animal in search of sustenance, they have fed their minds with a steady diet of new and useful information. This approach makes them smarter, more nimble, and better adapted to work in today's fast-paced workplace. We're all conditioned to the notion that corporate advancement is indexed to IQ scores—the smartest people get ahead. In reality, there's not a lot of evidence to support this premise. I've had more than a few brilliant people work for me who didn't have the necessary common sense or street smarts to excel in the workplace. There's a much stronger correlation between career success and the knowledge base someone has built within their profession. Over the years, thousands of scientists have tried to create an artificial intelligence computer. For my money, I'd rather have a regular computer with a database with all the answers. The same goes for my employees. I rarely find myself wishing I had a genius with a 150 IQ to help me solve a problem, although I'm constantly wanting someone who has taken the time to research our competitors' products, sought out the opinion of a customer about a critical issue, or is up on the latest trends in a market segment.

You need to think of your mind as a very capable computer. Take Ray Kurzweil as an example. He is one of the world's foremost computer scientists and one of the leading experts on artificial intelligence. He recently set out to determine the computer processing capacity that would be required to mimic the capability of the human brain. In his book, *The Age of Spiritual Machines*, he estimated that the human brain is capable of twenty million billion calculations per second, far more capable than any computer ever contemplated by man. (Today's 3Ghz Pentium computer performs three billion calculations per second, which doesn't come close to one percent of the computing power in your brain.) The computer on your shoulders can sort and utilize tremendous amounts of data—written, verbal, or visual. Now the important part is that it's severely underutilized without a vast database with which to operate.

Here's an image that might help you. I once knew a superstar employee who excelled in being well-informed. George was, and continues to be, a very successful executive and a great role model for the rest of us. Over the years, he developed outstanding information consumption habits. If you looked in his briefcase, you would almost always see a few industry journals and magazines that he reads when he has free time, like while waiting for a plane or sitting in a doctor's office waiting for an appointment. He regularly receives an email news clipping service, which scans the news wires for information pertinent to his job, company, and industry. George has ferreted out a few Internet discussion sites that discuss developments in his industry long before they appear in the traditional trade press. He realizes the need for deeper levels of understanding and reads a few books a year on topics related to his field. If you searched his Palm Pilot, you would see that his address book includes a large number of notations about the people he meets. His routine is to add new contacts to his address book, including his mental notes about them, whether they are colleagues, customers, business partners, or acquaintances. His notes often include spouse's and children's names, interests, and favorite sports teams. George's business contacts are always impressed when he remembers their children's names, when he congratulates them when their favorite team wins the championship, or when he remembers their last conversation. George enhances his overall business knowledge base by starting the day thirty minutes early so he can read the *Wall Street Journal* and reads two or three business magazines through the month. Incidentally, he picked one of those magazines because he knows it's a favorite of the company's president. Lastly, early in his career, George learned that it's virtually impossible to learn when your mouth is open; thus, he's taught himself to be a good listener and observer. When George attends meetings, he's learned to enjoy hearing varying perspectives and tries hard not to form his own opinions until he has heard what everyone has to say. Incidentally, George's information funnel costs him a few hundred dollars a year, which he views as a reasonable investment in himself.

So what has this vast store of information done for George? His company considers him one of the top brains within their ranks. He's perceived to be an expert on the industry and the competition and is often trusted with high-profile assignments. This happens because his depth of knowledge conveys a sense of confidence and trust. People enjoy interacting with him, because he can always be counted on to bring a fresh and interesting perspective. George is exceptional at bringing new ideas and concepts to his job, perhaps because he's exposed to so many sources of inspiration. He has figured out a way to pipeline his brain, which yields him a significant advantage among his peers.

If you're thinking all of this seems like a big time commitment, it depends on your perspective. George's job doesn't require him to do physical labor—like most of us, he's a knowledge worker. In the last century, your size, stature, and stamina played a large role in predicting your success in a career in agriculture, the dominant industry. Today, as a knowledge worker, it's what's in your brain that counts. Allocating a few hours per month toward feeding your brain is a prudent and worthwhile time investment in yourself and your career.

Connecting to the Information Spigot

The 1980s pundits were right: we're careening down the path to becoming an information society. While grains, bushels, and truck loads were the measures of yesterday's businesses, it's hard to find a modern profession that can't be boiled down to some form of human-assisted data manipulation. Whether you're an architect, a nurse, or a lawyer, chances are you spend the majority of your time interacting with information appliances, like personal computers and handhelds. And as if that isn't enough, in our free time, we devour other forms of digital content, whether on our iPods, Tivos, or home PCs. Information has become the new currency of our generation. If you have it, you've got the power. And if you don't, you're on the outside looking in.

It wouldn't be hard to become overwhelmed by the streams of information that flood our consciousness every day. While our parents may think we're hopelessly uninformed because we don't contribute to global deforestation by consuming a daily newspaper, they have no way of knowing that we're digesting ten times more information than they ever did. The hundreds of web pages, blogs, emails, and instant messages are just the start for most us. Slowly but surely we're becoming an evolved species, one that has a new specialization: the ability to filter and act on huge amounts of information.

Here are a few tips that can help you best make use of the Internet to build your store of knowledge:

1. **Select a few daily surfing links.**
   In your web browser you can bookmark a series of web pages that you can surf to as your beginning and end of the day news scan. (In Internet Explorer and Firefox you can put these links on your links toolbar, which will make this even easier and faster.) This list might include a few industry-specific news sites and a blog focused on your area of expertise. This quick scan capability will keep you abreast of breaking news for your industry.

2. **Use a few news alerts.**
   If you visit Google or Yahoo, it's easy to create a free daily or weekly news clipper that will automatically email you when a particular topic is reported in the press. If, for example, you want to be informed when there's news about your competitor, you simply define a news alert with its name or product in the alert. Google's news alerts are particularly easy to use. You can access them on the Google news page.

3. **Seek out commentary.**
   Here's a dirty little secret about the Internet: many of the reporters for Internet sites are among the most junior people within the press. Most websites don't pay well because they don't have significant revenues, therefore they can only afford junior people. Try to counterbalance your Internet news consumption with more expert commentary from the seasoned pros. If you search hard enough on the Web you'll find regular columns from opinion leaders, with the growing trend being on their own blogs.

Good Learning Habits

What can you do to develop your intellectual curiosity? You can start by not giving into the reflex that says "it's somebody else's job to understand that." Make it your business to understand how things work, what drives the business, or why an initiative is failing. Don't be content to simply understand a competitor's product; marvel at it. Look at it from every angle, and try to figure out its relative strengths and weaknesses. If your job requires you to service customers, commit yourself to learning something about the customer's company and industry.

Here are a few exercises that will help you develop this area of your brain:

• **Focus more on causes than effects**. The path of least resistance is to form opinions based on surface level observations. These lead us to say: "Joe is such a jerk," "That product sucks," or "They are really a tough competitor." Each of these observations is the result of a cause and effect relationship. Something happened that causes us to form an opinion. The bigger question is what's *causing* Joe to be such a jerk? Is there something going on in his life that's making him act this way? Has his boss unwittingly created an environment that encourages this behavior? What's *causing* the product to do so poorly in the market? Is the problem with its pricing or packaging? Are the marketing messages not resonating with the customer? It's one thing to tell me that our competitor is really tough and it's another to show me that your curiosity has led you to figure out that the competitor is spending more on training programs or that it's licensing some special sauce technology from another company.

- **Value varying perspectives.** As a general rule, we're not learning when we're playing defense. While your instinctive reaction might be to defend your point of view, your better option is make it a point to hear as many perspectives as possible. This way, you're benefiting from the combined brain power of everyone in the process. It's easy to find ourselves falling into the trap of matching wits with other smart people. When someone offers a conflicting view about something that is garnering your passion, and our fight-or-flight reflex says "fight."

  The better plan would be to simply listen to every perspective you can garner, with the hope that there are a few valuable points you can distill from the process. The next time you're watching a professional or big-time college basketball game, notice what happens when there's a timeout. A great coach follows a similar formula: before going into the huddle with the players, he'll first hold a huddle with his assistant coaches. The head coach will query his assistants by asking: "What are you seeing?" It's not until he has heard everyone's perspective that he will go into the huddle with players to address the team.

- **Learn from the experiences of experts.** If you're not reading a few autobiographies every year, you're missing a big learning opportunity. When a well-known business person, politician, or scientist takes the time to tell you about their career, it often yields a wealth of transferred knowledge. These books can be as valuable as the trendy how-to business book of the moment. It works like a type of learning osmosis: these new ideas and perspectives begin to permeate your consciousness, expanding your thought processes.

• **Make time for deep learning.** While you probably are reading thousands of words every day, I'm betting that most of them are gained by scanning and skimming at the superficial level. This is okay, but you need to supplement this information consumption with deeper learning experiences. Reading the commentary found on the editorial pages will give you new perspectives on newsworthy events. It's one thing to read an article on the Middle East and another to read a book about the origins of the conflict.

Career learning isn't too different from any other personal development undertaking. If your goal is to get in better physical shape, you already know that you'll need a disciplined program of exercise and good nutrition. If you want to build brain power, you need a similar approach: a structured process to build and feed your knowledge base. The medical data isn't ambiguous: mental capacity is self-developed and not a gift of genetics. Once you develop good learning habits, you'll find that more efficient learning becomes a way of life. Your well-developed intellectual curiosity will positively change the way you're perceived and give you much greater career satisfaction.

Chapter 7
Communicating with Clarity

Good communication is as stimulating as black coffee,
and just as hard to sleep after.

—*Anne Morrow Lindbergh (1906-2001), American writer and aviator*

After "What should I do with my life?" and "How can I make more money?" the next most frequent question I hear in my coaching activities is "How can I stand out as someone who brings my 'A' game to work?" We'd all like to be recognized for our skills and accomplishments, and there's nothing more frustrating than being passed over for an important assignment or position. When it seems like we couldn't give the company another ounce of our focus and energy, happy-go-lucky Joe gets that coveted new role. It leaves us wondering what we're doing wrong and how we can draw attention to our core strengths. So, what can you do to differentiate yourself from the crowd? While wearing black every day of his life worked for Johnny Cash, that's not what I had in mind. If you have a father who irritates you by telling you to "speak up and defend yourself" or "walk in and demand that job," this chapter will help you figure out how. *Honing your basic communication skills will make you a standout among your peers.* In this chapter, we'll address how you can do just that.

The Competent Communicator

Let's start by agreeing that recognition isn't demanded, it's earned. When executives look at the people in their organizations, they form opinions based on the interactions they have with them. Sure you might get a gold star for writing a riveting product positioning paper, but if you can't present it in a clear manner your brilliance is likely to be severely discounted. We still live in a people-to-people society, and your ability to communicate clearly will play a significant role in how far you go in your career and life.

The corporate organism is a complex beast. You take a problem, say making pharmaceuticals, and divide it into 25,000 pieces, each manned by a human being. Everyone is responsible for their 1/25,000th of the work, with a high degree of mutual dependence. Any one person can make (a scientist with a discovery) or break (a corrupt accountant) the mission of the firm. And what's the central nervous system of the company? Communication. Twenty-five thousand people working independently in a vacuum simply wouldn't succeed. The interactions we have in person, over the phone, and via electronic methods act as a binding agent in the corporate glue. All those conversations, meetings, and emails unite the company's individuals in a collective that's greater than the sum of its parts.

So when people ask me how they can stand out, I tell them first and foremost to be a good communicator. Nothing captivates a boss more than a young person who can dazzle the audience in a presentation, deliver a succinct verbal status update, or write a well-worded customer letter. The competent communicator instills a tremendous amount of confidence in his colleagues. He appears highly capable. It's great to possess above-average intelligence, but it's even better if you can convey your intelligence in a clear, engaging way. Virtually every position within the corporate hierarchy has multiple communications touch points—superiors, colleagues, customers, and vendors—who all present an opportunity for you to draw attention (either positively or negatively) to your capabilities.

Face Time

Where can you start improving in this critical area? The first place that often has room for improvement is dealing with people instead of machines. As one of today's young professionals, you are someone who is facile with modern communications technologies; email, voice mail, and instant messaging have always been a part of your work lives. While these technologies have done much to speed the flow of corporate information, they've also served to diminish the quality of human interactions. Unfortunately, the majority of people have become more adept at communicating through a machine than face-to-face, person-to-person. We all know the verbose, emotional emailer who is a reticent church mouse in department meetings. Her trepidation is obvious when she's forced to speak up, as if she is saying, "Can't we solve this with an email thread?" To a manager, it's easy to look at these people as corporate monks. There's no self-imposed pressure to move these people to higher levels of authority.

I was once in a customer-save meeting attempting to salvage one of our best accounts from falling into the hands of our competition. This customer was upset with our company and had put us on notice that he was considering dropping us. We had representatives from most of the customer-facing departments at the meeting, including sales, customer service, accounting, and product engineering. The atmosphere was tense since no one wanted to see our best flagship customer leave the fold—nor did anyone want to be responsible for this loss. Everyone was trying to decide which way to go: constructive or CYA (cover your ass). As the CEO, my appearance served to underscore the importance of saving this showcase account.

For the first three quarters of the meeting, each department presented its chronology of the situation. The customer support people presented the problem history along with the corrective measures they'd tried; engineering explained the nature of the bug and what was being done to remedy the problem; accounting discussed the invoice issues and the back-and-forth they had with the customer when he refused to pay our bills. From a purely mechanical perspective, the problem resolution machinery was working in a textbook fashion. Everyone seemed to have their hearts and mind in the right place, but somehow this customer hated us and wanted to sever our relationship. What was going on?

I had visited this customer on several occasions, and now something in the back of my mind was saying "things aren't adding up." Time for a few questions. After about an hour of this departmental reporting process, I posed a simple question to the group: "Are we talking to this customer?" The customer service representative assigned to the customer defensively said, "I've talked to this customer one or more times a day for the past two weeks." There were several nods and "me too's" around the table, which made me pose the question differently: "I mean, are we *really* talking to this customer? You know...picking up the phone and having human-to-human conversations? Or better yet, have we gotten into our cars and driven out to see this customer?" The oh-shit looks I was getting from everyone confirmed my suspicions, and it was then that I started extracting confessions from the group. It seems the "talking" we had been doing with the customer was largely through email and instant messaging. In fact, it was clear to me that we had not conducted a person-to-person meeting with this customer since the last time the salesperson sold them something. A customer who was paying us more than $100,000 per year was on the receiving end of instant messaging snippets? No wonder we were in the doghouse.

Face-to-face communication is quickly becoming a lost art—and an opportunity for you. There are far too many people who are more comfortable typing messages into a machine than interacting human-to-human. As the CEO of a company, I'm often the recipient of an email thread that started several days before I'm asked to weigh in with an opinion. When I start from the bottom and read through all the messages, it makes me want to scream. I'm thinking, "Can't you people just get in a room or on a conference call and solve this problem like humans?" The amount of wasted energy that comes from email ping-pong is approaching astronomical levels. (For more tips on appropriate use of email, see the section entitled "Living in the Electronic Age" later in this chapter.)

There's still a certain warmth and feeling that only comes when we're *really* talking with someone. Take away the backspace key and the emoticons and add the resonance of a human voice, the facial expressions and gestures, and you've got the formula for a higher order of interaction. If you want to stand out among your peers, my first advice is to master the lost art of traditional human interaction. In this multi-megabyte, high-bandwidth world, you'll stand out like a midget who can dunk. The population of young professionals who speak, present, and converse well is shrinking at the rate that email use is growing. Pick up the phone, make an appointment, call a meeting—anything but another round of corporate spam. The potential dividends to your career are huge.

The Art of Clarity

Okay, so you've decided to drop the keyboard and have a face-to-face meeting about something crucial happening at work. What can you do to make the meeting more beneficial for you? The best of the best are people who can distill complex and gnarly issues to their very essence. They have a knack for explaining things in a way that everyone can understand. In much the same way that Stephen Hawkins makes the universe digestible for the 99.99 percent of the population that didn't study astrophysics, they get their points across where others fail. Concise and articulate people who can crystallize complex topics are an essential, and typically well-paid, entity within the corporate communications structure.

Here are a few secrets that the gifted communicator employs to get his points across:

1. Three is a magic number.

Typically, people aren't capable of digesting more than three concurrent thoughts at one time. Saying, "Boss, there are three things we need to do to put the project back on-track," is far better than saying, "Let me take you through the twelve-point improvement plan." The rule of three extends across the entire spectrum of communications. If you start a meeting by saying you have three objectives for the meeting, your participants will find it easy to focus in on your plan.

2. Be prepared.

At the root of most nervousness and discomfort is a lack of preparation. Someone once told me a secret for preparing for interviews that you can extend to almost any one-on-one meeting that makes you nervous. Instead of deliberating about the answers he would give, he would write down all of the questions he thought he'd likely be asked. Next, he would write down the answers to the questions in bulleted form. This type of preparation yields amazing results. Rather than responding with ums and ahhs as you think through your answers, you'll come off as crisp and articulate as your prepared responses pop into your brain. This approach works equally well for presentations, contentious meetings, and Q&A sessions.

3. Keep things simple.

While you might be tempted to impress your listener with your vast wealth of knowledge, your best approach is to ensure he understands the essence of the message. If you listen to a good politician making his pitch, you'll observe that it's plain-speak without the under-the-surface mumbo jumbo that underpins the legislative process. Instead of saying, "The caucus committee needs to reach a consensus on the appropriation," he'll say, "My colleagues and I will work together to get you the money you need." I've spent most of my life developing computer hardware and software, and I always use my mother as a benchmark: if I can't explain my latest project in a way that she understands it, I'm not simplifying enough.

4. If you are a nervous public speaker, run, don't walk, to your nearest Toastmasters Club meeting and sign up.

Toastmasters is a non-profit organization with a singular mission: to help people become better public speakers. At any one time, more than 200,000 people are involved in more than 9,000 clubs, all on a personal improvement mission. It's cheap, it's been proven effective by thousands of corporate executives, and it's a lot of fun. You can get more information at www.toastmasters.org.

5. In written communications, use this tried-and-true method.

Tell the recipient what you are going to say, say it, then tell them what you just told them. It might look something like this:

Dear Boss,

I am writing to give you an update on the Polaris Project. As of last night, everything is on-track towards the production of widgets. We have three major steps left; they are: 1.) completing the first production run; 2.) debugging the process; and 3.) finalizing the ramp-up to full capacity.

I thought you'd like to hear the project is on track. Let me know if you need more information.

Sincerely,
Kathy

Keep your communications short and on-point. The recipient will appreciate it, and your career will benefit from it.

Living in the Electronic Age

Although the emphasis in communications should always be on establishing frequent face time, electronic communiqués are unavoidable in this age. As discussed, email is ubiquitous in the modern workplace, and when used appropriately it can help extend the business day and allow us to accomplish simple tasks using short messages. When used as a crutch to replace one-on-one time, it can dull our person-to-person skills and make us look meek to our superiors, customers, and colleagues. Here are a few tips to keep your email use in the acceptable zone:

1. **Remember that email is a messaging medium, not a conversation medium**. If the email message is going to be more than one paragraph, pick up the phone or walk down the hall. Most people don't take time to read long messages, and if they do, it results in a long reply you don't want to read. Or, worse yet, they haven't fully comprehended all you were trying to convey anyway and your message is misunderstood. Proctor and Gamble, for instance, has long had a prohibition on corporate memos that exceed one page.

2. **Be judicious on your use of the reply-to-all button.** We all like to look like the smart guy, so we reply to everyone...although, in reality it often serves to stoke the flame mail cycle. You need only reply to the key figures that should be in-the-know on the issue. Also, if your reply is potentially contentious, you should start by telling your correspondent that you've only sent the response to him. Flame mail (an email tirade you receive with many people copied on the distribution list) is an act perpetrated by insecure people. Take away their audience and the venom will disappear.

3. **Don't send emails down the hall, to the next cube, or to your boss located in the same building.** It's easier and more effective to see them in person. If you need to maintain a paper trail for verification purposes, ensure that

you sum up the decision/plan/whatever and send the message in only one email—not a series.

4. **Never, ever, ever, express anger in electronic form.** I can only guarantee you a sleepless night filled with regret after launching your well-intentioned tirade. Not one angry emailer hasn't wanted to rescind a message written in haste and anger. Like it or not, email is a more permanent medium than print. Why? Because your message can be forwarded, archived, and retrieved from now until the archaeologists are digging up our civilization.

5. **Take time to answer the question of whether your email is something you'd want to be around forever.** While that off-color joke seemed worthy of forwarding, it might not appear so innocent to a plaintiff's attorney who's trying to dig-up material for a discrimination suit—whether or not you are the accused.

Early in my career I worked in an office where a disgruntled employee brought a suit of this type against the company. Within days his lawyers convinced a judge to require copies of every memo and email for everyone in the department. More than a few people were concerned about their seemingly innocent emails being taken out of context. Do you really want to be sitting in a room with your company's defense attorneys answering questions about the off-color video file you forwarded—especially when your actions stand to hurt their defense of a million-dollar discrimination suit? Here's how the process works in the real world. When your company gets sued, the very first thing on the plaintiff's list of discovery (the things the judge will allow them to see) will be the back-up tapes from your corporate email system. Next, the attorneys will run a scanning program that will use keywords to ferret out those emails that potentially support their case. If they are trying to prove that your company had an environment that encouraged inappropriate behavior, your email will now be used in the chain of evidence. Is forwarding that joke worth the career-damaging aggravation? Seemingly innocent replies to emails, like "good one" or "very funny," are great ammunition for the plaintiff's bar. We all have a friend who sends these things with regularity. Do yourself and your career a favor; pick up the phone, and tell him "please don't send these messages to my work address."

6. **It has become vogue to send emails lacking capital letters, punctuation, and properly spelled words.** Sometimes these come from a higher-up who's trying to say, "I'm too busy to send anything but streams of thought" or "I'm informal and don't want to seem too stuffy, so I'm going to skip using proper punctuation." While insulting to your correspondent, it also ignores the fact that emails get stored and forwarded. It's much better to look like a formal traditionalist than have your stream of consciousness email forwarded beyond your intended target.

One additional email tip: use the size of a computer screen as a measurement tool to gauge your level of brevity. A good rule of thumb is to make sure your message won't roll off the receiver's computer screen. Email has become a scan and triage medium, and with ever-higher volumes we have no choice but to become adept at triage. Virtually everyone does the same thing with a verbose lengthy email—they skip with the unrealistic goal of coming back to it later. The problem is that tomorrow's one hundred emails will come in on top of it, burying it to the land of never seen again.

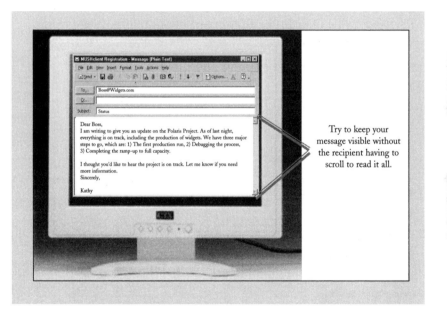

Try to keep your message visible without the recipient having to scroll to read it all.

Communicating with Your Boss

Interacting with your boss should be a top priority of your job. The advantages of a good relationship with your boss are numerous. One of your objectives should be to improve your face time with your boss. First and foremost: bring him answers, not questions. As a manager, it's very exasperating to be approached by an employee with a problem that isn't well thought through. It's as if they are saying, "I'm too lazy to use my own brain cells, so I'd like to use some of yours." Chances are the manager has her own long list of problems to solve, thus adding a new load isn't an attractive prospect.

Here's how the star employee does it. He starts the meeting by saying, "I'm really stuck on the alpha project. I've given it a lot of thought, and I think we have three potential courses of action we can take to put it back on-track. I need your help in choosing option A, B, or C." Even if his manager doesn't agree with the potential options, she'll be impressed that the person has given the problem a lot of thought and that he is brave enough to recommend a course of action. Your boss pays you to bring him answers, not questions.

Another way you can improve communications with your manager is to keep your interactions within the context of his mission. I've had more than a few employees who viewed my role as psychotherapist. One in particular used to dump on me all the time about her stresses, trials, and tribulations. While I'm sure it made her feel better, it made me feel like she was in over her head. If you really want to get on my good side, you'll always make me feel like you are a stakeholder in *my* success.

I look at my world in simple terms: my boss measures me on ability to achieve a certain outcome, and each of my eight people owns one eighth of this problem. Before we get to all the nice-nice and happy talk, I need to feel like your actions are 100 percent targeted towards helping me achieve this goal. Your taking vacation during a critical time or whining to me about how stressed you are won't engender this belief.

Instead of wasting your time telling me about your inability to get a meeting set up at Clark Corp., I'd rather you spend it describing your contingency plans for helping me achieve my number. Similarly, don't waste my time complaining about someone in another department; tell me a new idea that will help us succeed.

A Ticket to Greater Things

Standing out as a top performer begins with something nearly all of us learned to do before we were a year old: communicate. No matter how brilliant your brain or how many hours you work, if you cannot clearly convey your thoughts, you will not be effective in any position. If you feel your communication skills aren't as polished as they should be, be proactive about improving them. At work, pay close attention to the executives at your next divisional meeting. Examine how they conduct the meeting, and learn from their example. Try taking a course at your local community college, such as Business Writing, or join a public speaking organization or even an improv group. Sometimes we need to go back to the basics in order to advance.

Chapter 8
Superior People Skills

Power comes not from the barrel of a gun but from one's
awareness of his or her own cultural strength
and the unlimited capacity to empathize with, feel for, care,
and love one's brothers and sisters.

—*Addison Gayle, Jr. (1932-1991), American educator, critic, and author*

Much is made of the differences in style among
professionals. Over the years, I've had the good fortune
to know thousands of business people, from entry-level college
grads to CEOs of large companies. From the high-pressure
type-A to the passively analytical, I've seen a pretty good cross
section of the various flavors of people. *In observing them, I've
consistently seen one personality trait that seems to serve as an
important indicator of success in the business world.* It seems to
transcend the stereotypes: hard-chargers who don't have it
flounder and mild-mannered analytical types who possess it
can progress through their pyramids very quickly. This one
trait seems to cut broadly across the spectrum of professions,

personalities, and styles. The people who have it seem to ooze a level of charisma and self-confidence that says, "I can do it." The image in your mind is probably of that likable person who seems at-ease communicating with peers, bosses, and colleagues—and always seems to be on top of her game. This trait makes people *want* to work with them.

So what's the special sauce that serves to differentiate very successful people from the pack? Is it possible that one attribute could play such an important defining role? I'm certain the answer is yes. In fact, if you were offered the choice of twenty additional points on your Intelligence Quotient or this unique attribute, you should take the special sauce. So what is it? Cue the drum roll…in a word, it is:

Empathy

Webster's dictionary defines empathy as "the action of understanding, being aware of, being sensitive to, and vicariously experiencing the feelings, thoughts, and experience of another." In simple speak, it means being able to put yourself in someone else's shoes.

We traditionally think of empathy playing a role in our personal lives with our friends and loved ones. When a mother hugs a crying two-year-old with a skinned knee, she can *feel* the child's pain as if it is happening to her. Similarly, it doesn't take much effort to internalize the feelings of fear and anguish when you spend time at the bedside of a dying family member. And, who hasn't felt their own heart beating and palms sweating when a good friend walks up to the podium to deliver a public speech?

While this emotive form of empathy resides close to our heartstrings, it's also relevant in our professional lives. Have you ever been in a presentation when the person speaking isn't connecting with the audience? How about the nurse that doesn't appreciate that the patient lying in front of her is wondering if he's going to make it through the surgery? We've all experienced the customer service agent whose voice says, "I'm just here to answer the phone" rather than "I can imagine how frustrating it must be to have spent $500 on something that doesn't work."

One of my favorite illustrations of empathy took place in the movie *The Doctor.* The film starts by profiling a crack shot team of surgeons who were sufficiently self-impressed with their life-saving talents. The story takes an interesting turn when the obnoxious star surgeon, played by William Hurt, comes down with throat cancer. Seeing the world as a patient casts a new light on the fears, concerns, embarrassments, and emotional sensitivities of being a seriously ill patient surrounded by insensitive doctors. In the closing scene of the movie, the cured surgeon is seen rounding up the hotshot med students and handing them the flimsy open-backed night-gowns worn by patients. He informs them that the first step to becoming a good doctor is to be able to relate to patients and that they'll be wearing those gowns for the weekend.

Empathetic people have an ability to put themselves in someone else's shoes and adjust their thoughts, words, or actions to the situation. Former President Reagan was nick-named "The Great Communicator" for his consistent ability to tune his message to his audience. President Clinton was well known for his "I feel your pain" statement, mostly because he was convincing in his effort to convey that he really understood what it was like to be in *our* shoes. People with this learned ability have a tremendous edge in their human interactions. In many ways it's like they are playing a card game with x-ray eyes; they have a pretty good idea what's in the other player's hand. We've all seen examples of that perfect administrative assistant who always seems to be one step ahead of her boss. While some claim it's a matter of clairvoyance, I'd say she's an empathetic person.

Good listening skills and empathy are closely linked. In fact, you'll often hear psychologists talking about "empathic listening," which they use to describe a more engaged form of conversation. By putting himself in your shoes, the empathetic person can converse on a deeper, more involved level. It's one thing to hear your friend tell his story about a car accident and another to *live* it with him, imagining the uncontrolled feeling of terror as the car slid off the road, the eerie silence that followed the impact, and the fearful self-assessment that answers the question "am I in one piece?"

I once knew a salesperson who had a well developed level of empathy. If you met Mary in the grocery store, I'd bet you would not walk away thinking she was a world-class sales professional. She doesn't fit the aggressive/assertive stereotype, her closing skills are modest, and she's not known for putting in exceptionally long hours. Her results tell a different story: she is among the very best in her industry. Her secret? Mary has the well-honed ability to put herself in her customers' shoes and anticipate their concerns, interests, or needs. When I would sit down with Mary and ask her about the progress of a hotly contested sale, she would give me a thoughtful analysis of the situation.

For instance, she would say something like: "Joe is nervous to buy from us because we're a relatively new company, and everything around him says he doesn't like risk and he buys the tried and true solution. We need to speak to his reticence and see if we can get him comfortable that we too are a stable company that will be here for the long-term." Note that if you had planted a tape recording in the room with the customer, you would not have heard him say that he was concerned about the risks of doing business with the company. Instead, as Mary put herself in Joe's shoes and attempted to see life through his eyes, she rightly concluded that he was a risk-adverse guy. She saw herself in his situation, in his new job, reluctant to make an early mistake that would make him seem naïve. She observed that he drove a traditional car and preferred conservative attire. In taking in the whole picture, she noted that his children had traditional, versus trendy names, and that he still used a paper calendar. By putting herself in his shoes, she was able to accurately size up the situation and construct a go-forward approach.

While her competitor is sitting in front of the customer thinking about what to *say* next, Mary is "sitting" in the customer's chair envisioning what he's going to *think* next. When Mary entertains her customers, things seem to go incredibly smoothly, with her customers having this sense that she's one step ahead of them—because she is. She spends a lot of time putting herself in their shoes and has an instinct for what should come next. And during the difficult periods when her company or one her products fails to satisfy her customers, she knows the right things to say and the appropriate corrective actions to initiate before it becomes a crisis. She can do this because she knows their hot buttons and never lets things reach those levels.

Do You Need to Improve Your Empathy Skills?

People lacking empathy are often easy to spot. Here are a few warning signs that might indicate you have room for improvement in this area:

• **Excessive Use of the Words "I" and "Me" in Conversations**
  Empathetic people spend much of their time "in" the minds of their correspondent, leaving less time to talk about themselves. They understand that everyone likes talking about themselves and their interests; thus, they make it easy and comfortable for their colleagues to express themselves.

• **Friction in Relationships at Work**
  The person lacking in empathy often has antagonistic relationships outside of their work group or department. They fail to spend enough time understanding and appreciating other people's constraints and challenges; thus, they view any reluctance to help as being uncooperative. These people are much more likely to say something negative about a colleague than to appreciate the whole situation.

• **Surprise Endings and Outcomes**
  Because the person lacking empathy often engages at the

superficial level, he or she frequently misses the subtle nuances that reveal themselves when a project, sale, or relationship is off-track.

Difficult People: The Empathetic Approach

There is another area in which empathy can help you in your business dealings. One of the frustrating aspects of life in the workplace is dealing with the friction that sometimes arises between us and our colleagues. Conference room arguments, flame mail, and difficult people—talk about life stressors!— have become a part of the high-intensity workplace. It's important to note that very few people actually wake up in the morning and think: "I'm so glad it's Thursday; today's the day I'd like to really piss people off." It's usually something about the person's environment, measurement systems, or top-down direction that is making them act in a manner that you feel is unreasonable.

The next time you find yourself up against an uncooperative coworker, instead of letting the sparks and email fly, I advocate taking a different approach. Try putting yourself in your roadblock's shoes and figure out what's going on in his world that is making him act this way. Perhaps the salesperson that isn't returning your call is under immense pressure to bring in the month's orders. Perhaps a colleague's measurement systems run counter to what you are demanding. Would you volunteer to help someone if it meant blowing an important performance measurement metric? Or perhaps the systems person has been requesting tools to solve problems such as yours for months but can't get budget approval from her boss. Wouldn't that make you scream at the next person with whom you spoke?

(For additional approaches on how to deal with difficult people, please refer to Chapter 9: Corporate Combat.)

Empathy in Action

Someone once asked Larry King what makes him such a good interviewer. He responded by offering an example: "NBC News anchorman Tom Brokaw arrives at the scene of a blazing house fire just as a brave fireman, holding a small child, is coming out of a burning doorway. Brokaw sticks a microphone in the fireman's face and asks in a demanding voice: 'Was this fire arson?' As the stunned fireman is about to answer, Larry King sticks a microphone in the fireman's face and asks: 'Why did you want to be a fireman?'"

It's worth mentioning the importance of understanding how measurement systems affect our colleague's behaviors. In the rational world, people aspire to achieve the measurement objectives to which they are held. Salespeople want to make their quotas, air traffic controllers need to ensure that a majority of planes are running on time, engineers are focused on achieving their delivery dates and quality scores, lawyers need to bill a certain amount per month to uphold their responsibilities to their firm's partnership structure, and proofreaders need to find every mistake before a book goes to print. It's safe to say that the vast majority of people care about how they are measured, and they will go to great lengths to achieve their measurement objectives—including brushing aside someone whom they feel is extraneous to the achievement of these goals. In the spirit of leading the horse to water, you'll be better served understanding how someone is measured and demonstrating how your request will help him ultimately achieve his aims than expecting abject benevolence. Let's say you were the product manager for the iPod and you had a request for the lead product engineer to make a fundamental change to the main menu. This request would require a major software change, including a new quality assurance testing cycle. He's under the gun to get the next version of the iPod out, and your request is the last thing he wanted to hear. If you take the typical route, you'll send him an email, he'll bitch and moan, and you'll go whining to your boss that you can't get the cooperation you need. Here's another approach: "James, I have a request for you that might not be what you want to hear, although in the end it's a win-win for both of us. We are seeing a high number of product returns related to consumers getting stuck at a particular menu step. They think the product is broken, when in reality it's just a menu design problem. Since I'm measured on unit sales, and product returns count against your QA numbers, we should work together to make this change. Be assured, I'm open to any ideas you might have to make the process as painless as possible."

Empathy: Learning to Do It Better

A well-developed level of empathy will serve you well in almost all aspects of your professional life. Here are a few examples:

• **Negotiations**

The best negotiators I have known are empathetic students of their adversary. When you sit in the negotiation war room with one of these people, you realize that they are "in" their adversary's head. While plotting the next tactic or offer, you'll often hear them recite a thesis about what's going on in the other side's war room. They'll say something like: "He's an impatient guy who doesn't like uncertainty. Everything about him says he needs to feel in control of his world. We're at-risk because he might be getting tired of this process and views our competitor's offer as the shortest path to getting this off his desk. Let's go back to him with an offer to engage in a twenty-four-hour exclusive negotiating period then bring all the right people in one room— with a mutual commitment that no one leaves until we have a deal or no-deal decision. And tell him we can be there at 8:00 a.m. tomorrow."

These talented and empathetic negotiators often spend as much time thinking about the other side's thoughts and emotions as well as their own, giving them a huge tactical advantage.

• **Customer/Client Service and Support**

Empathy often separates the average customer service person from the great customer service person. Is there anything more frustrating than dealing with a customer service person who can't relate to the problem you are experiencing? The average customer service rep delivers service by the book with a mechanical commitment to closing the trouble ticket, thus adding to their measurement scorecard. The great rep puts himself in your shoes, appreciates the let-down of a dead-on-arrival product, and conveys a level of concern that starts to make you feel better. He can clearly picture what it must be like to have a product disappoint you after so much anticipation. His words, tonality, and resourcefulness say: "I understand, I care, and I'm on your side."

I was once traveling with a female colleague who realized too late that she had forgotten to pack matching hose for her next day's outfit. On the way from the airport to the hotel she stopped at Nordstrom's right before closing only to find that they didn't have her size in the right color. The sales clerk offered to try other stores, although my employee informed her that she'd be leaving town the next morning. Resigned to a poorly dressed reality, she made her way to the hotel empty-handed. At 8:00 the next morning her phone rang. It was the Nordstrom rep, who was now in the hotel lobby. She said that she could sense the urgency of the situation, so she drove across town on her way home the previous night and picked up a pair of matching hose. A very empathetic moment.

• Public Speaking

The best public speakers I know are students of their audiences. As they are preparing for their speech, they want to know as much as possible about their audience, so they can tune their tone and message to the listener. I once worked for a senior executive who could parachute into a city, breeze into an auditorium full of disgruntled customers or employees, and nail a talk that would disarm the masses and leave them feeling good about a situation that had been festering for months. It wasn't until I was senior enough to be the person charged with picking him up at the airport and taking him to the meeting did I learn his secret. His airport-to-office routine was well-honed: he'd pummel me for the first forty minutes of the ride with questions about the audience then spent the last ten minutes in reflective silence. He'd ask me questions like "What's on their minds?" "What do they need to hear?" "What would make them feel better?" By the time he walked into the room, he could put himself in their shoes and leave no one thinking that he didn't have a handle on the situation.

• **Deal-Making**
When it comes to striking a deal—whether it's a major purchase like a car or house, investing in a company, settling a legal matter, or entering into a partnership arrangement— virtually everyone's emotions can be distilled down to a simple balancing act: the fear of missing out on a good deal versus the fear of doing a bad one. Often the fear of doing a bad deal is the dominant emotion since no one likes to be made the fool. People who are good at striking deals, and thus bringing the other side over to their position, take an empathetic approach to tilting the balance towards the fear of missing out. They speak to your emotions, helping you understand that there's more risk of missing out on a good deal than doing a bad one. An empathetic real estate agent might say: "These decisions are always stressful. After all, it may be the largest purchase you'll ever make. You are right to take a careful and thoughtful approach. As you're thinking about it, keep in mind that historically houses in this neighborhood have doubled in value

every five years, which explains why these houses are never on the market for very long."

Before	After
"I"	"You"
How are you doing?	What are you trying to accomplish?
What do you do for a living?	What are your passions?
Win-lose relationship	Win-win relationship
He's such a jerk	Nobody wants to suck at their job

I believe empathy is a learned, not inherited, trait. There are concrete actions you can take to strengthen this human-to-human attribute. Here are a few exercises to improve your empathy fitness level:

• **Teach Yourself to Talk *with* People**

In the busy world in which we live, it has become easier to talk *at* people instead of *with* them. The next time you're at a cocktail party, sit back and observe the conversations going on around you. Most will be the superficial variety, with the parties trying to steer the conversation to their interest area or towards a graceful exit. The typical cocktail party banter is a process of people talking *at* versus *with* each other. Rather than dealing on this superficial level, teach yourself to truly engage with the person. Listen to what the person is saying, and ask him questions that speak to his emotions. Observe his face, mannerisms, and dress, and try to imagine life as this person. One important tip to remember: concentrate on leaving the words "I" and "me" out of conversations—they tend to bring conversations to a disinteresting end. Here's an example of two very different conversations between coworkers:

Talking *at* Each Other

> You: Were you on vacation last week? I left you a message but didn't hear back.
>
> Joe: Yes, we went to the Bahamas.
>
> You: I went there once.
>
> Joe: When?
>
> You: When I was in college.
>
> Joe: Oh, where did you go to college?
>
> You: Florida State.
>
> (Yawn)

Talking *with* Someone

> You: Were you on vacation last week? I looked for you at the departmental lunch on Wednesday.
>
> Joe: Yes. My wife and I went to the Bahamas.
>
> You: It must have felt great to escape this cold winter.
>
> Joe: Yes, it was great to get away.
>
> You: So, what did you do when you were there? Any sight-seeing or did you just take some time to relax?
>
> Joe: We did a little of both. We spent a couple of days on the beach and took a couple of tours. I've got lots of photos. Care to see them?
>
> You: Sure, love to.

• **Study Strangers**

A good way to exercise your empathy muscle is teach yourself to be more sensitive to the people around you. The next time you are in the subway or waiting in line at the bank, practice studying the people around you. Look at their faces and try to imagine what's going through their minds. Envision life as this person, both the good and bad. Imagine what the person was like as a small child and what it must have been like to grow up in her shoes.

• **Prepare for Your Business Interactions**

Before sitting down to meet with someone, take a few moments to put yourself in the shoes of this person. Try and imagine what's going on in his world. Ask yourself these questions:

1. If I were in her shoes, what would I be thinking before coming to this meeting?
2. What negative preconceived notions would I have?
3. What life stressors do I have?
4. What would be my definition of a good meeting?

The answers to these questions might put you in a different frame of mind as you open up the discussion. You might start out with an objective of overcoming his concerns, versus giving your pitch.

Strengthening your empathy techniques will serve you well in your business life. While the world is becoming increasingly technologically advanced, most business interactions still boil down to people dealing with people. Being adept at interacting with people is still a very desirable attribute. Before long you'll be able to think like your boss, colleagues, and customers, resulting in win-win interactions and relationships.

Chapter 9
Corporate Combat

People prefer to follow those who help them,
not those who intimidate them.

—*C. Gene Wilkes (1798-1877), U.S. naval officer who*
explored the region of Antarctica named for him

Early in my career I was promoted to a job in France
working for one of Hewlett-Packard's manufacturing
divisions. As a product manager, my job was to be the human
interface between the sales force and our division's research,
development, and manufacturing operations. When I started
in this position, everyone warned me that the worst part of the
job would be dealing with the production manager in the
manufacturing department. They told me that he was the
most cantankerous guy in the company with a love for
chewing out product managers loudly and often. The problem
was I needed to speak with this guy every week during a
regular meeting. Among my key responsibilities was to assess
our worldwide sales force's demand and translate it into an
order forecast for him. With this data, he could order the

appropriate parts and schedule the necessary labor to fill the orders. In theory, we were supposed to be a team.

He lived up to his well-deserved reputation during our first telephone call. He unloaded on me about how worthless product managers were and made it clear that he considered my predecessor a failure. He bitched about the poor forecasts he'd been receiving and made it clear that he wouldn't have a lot of time for me. During his five-minute diatribe, it took every ounce of energy to contain my Irish temper. While I really wanted to tell this guy to eat something my editor won't let me print in this book, my better judgment told me that this wouldn't be the best method to announce my presence within HP France. I bit my tongue, muddled through the call, resolving to give this situation some thought. I was quite sure I didn't want to spend the next few years of my life being kicked around by this corporate ignoramus.

As I was driving home that night, I considered things from his point of view (using my empathetic skills). What was going on in his life that made him mow people down like that? And what could I do to tame this beast? In a perfect world, everyone in the workplace would be courteous, helpful, and respectful. We'd pull on the oars together as a team, and we'd all share the credit for our successes. As we know, the corporation isn't this perfect world, and dealing with difficult people situations is part of life in the workplace. Fortunately (for my hairline), I was able to find a way to work with my French colleague. In building the bridge to him, I learned that my predecessor had never visited the factory where he worked, and he often escalated things to his boss. The picture was starting to make sense. I committed myself to spending time at the factory, to understanding this guy's job, and paying particular attention to how he was measured. I also wanted to make sure he knew what my job was about and how I got an "A" with my boss. As is often the case, as soon as we met face-to-face, when I was no longer an over-the-phone punching bag, he became a rational person. In the end, we had a great working relationship with the moral of the story being the energy you invest in the early part of a relationship will pay off over time.

The workplace is a complex, politically charged environment, made more so by the diversity and passions of the participants. Office politics, dealing with difficult people, and the rumor mill all make the workplace a more stressful place. While we're rowing the corporate advancement boat as hard as we can, it's those undercurrents which toss us about. Ambition drives many people, and if it's at your expense, that's just a casualty of the game of corporate combat. In this chapter we will discuss the techniques you can employ to deal with the difficult situations that are a part of corporate life.

Dealing with Difficult People

When I have a bad day at the office I often tell my wife that work would be great if it wasn't for the people. I'm quite sure that my most and least favorite parts of my career have been the people. Hanging out with really smart people who are easy to get along with is a blast. The great people that I've been teamed up with over the years make up the best-of highlight reel in that plays in my mind. I can't remember what my offices looked like or the colors of my desks, but the great times with my colleagues are indelible memories in my mind. Conversely, I can still elevate my blood pressure, on command, when I reflect on the difficult people who have crossed my path. Their words, actions, and tactics can still gnaw at me weeks, months, and years later.

Difficult people come in all flavors, although there are three particular flavors that are especially destructive. The people who fit these top three stereotypes are the ones that seem to add the most stress to an organization. Their behaviors can drive the best and brightest people to their wits end, leaving a wake of stress, dismay, and frustration in their path. Who are these people? Allow me to introduce The Intimidator, The Obstructionist, and Mr. Ambition.

The Intimidator

We all know the type. He's usually in management; he's stern, abrupt, and unapproachable. He's got a reputation for being smart but no-nonsense. Often he has physical stature on his side, adding to his imposing image. I once knew one of these guys, and he had knives tattooed on his hands—apparently from his days as a Navy Seal. His presence in a meeting room put a chill in the air, and the smart money in the office pool said he wouldn't smile anytime in the next six months. How do you deal with someone like this?

Let's start by saying The Intimidator is almost always an insecure person. Rather than exhibiting the classic traits of the secure person—a self-depreciating sense of humor, approachability, and empathy—he chooses to erect walls that protect him from having to reveal his weaknesses. This personality style is the office version of the playground bully. He knows he's intimidating everyone, and he's perfectly happy to have this barrier around his faults.

What are the secrets to working with people like this? Forget about trying to win him over; this guy doesn't want friends. There's no thorn you can pull from his paw that will make him a sympathetic creature. Rather than making a friend, focus your energies earning this person's respect. Once he knows he can intimidate a person, he'll push that button anytime he's starting to feel insecure about himself. Making you feel uncomfortable makes him feel better, get it? On the other hand, if The Intimidator knows he can't knock you off your game through intimidation, he's likely to have a healthy respect for you. And what's the best way to demonstrate your lack of fear of him? Competence through preparation.

Often the root cause of feeling intimidated is the fear that you'll be caught off-guard without the right answer. Compounding this natural fear is a little voice saying: "I don't know how to communicate with this beast." The sure-fire way to beat back these irrational fears is with a little pre-meeting preparation.

Here's an example. Let's say that your project team nominated you to go speak with the company's curmudgeonly chief financial officer about the budget parameters for the project. Your first instinct is to send him an email, although your better judgment says to meet him in person. His secretary arranges for you to come to his office for a 7:30 a.m. meeting the following week. As you set the phone down after making this appointment, you can feel your stomach churning and your palms sweating. This guy has a reputation for chewing up newbies and spitting them out. You make a mental note to buy some antacids when you're at the store. (Incidentally, not only is your nervousness natural, it's an essential part of the process.)

Here's an approach that will help you with the meeting:

Step 1: Create an agenda for the meeting with no more than three items. It should be composed of something like: 1.) Bringing the CFO up-to-date on the project; 2.) The budget challenges he faces; and 3.) Understanding the mid-year budgeting feasibility for the project. Having an agenda will keep you both on-track as well as provide you with a template to guide your pre-meeting preparation.

Step 2: Prepare a one-page brief that you can use to present your three agenda topics (remember the rule of three!), as well as something you can leave behind to jar his memory about what you need from him. You're going to be pointing at this document, so I recommend a bulleted outline versus a wordy narrative.

Step 3: A common mistake people make is to jump right into the meat of the conversation without taking the time for a little ice-breaking. Prepare your opening small talk, which will serve to relieve the natural tension that exists at the beginning of every meeting. It's very difficult to have a productive meeting when the air is charged with unhelpful task tension. Don't talk about last Sunday's Rams game; instead, focus your small talk on a non-controversial business topic. You might ask him his opinion about a recent acquisition in your industry or a move by one of your competitors. Just be sure to be ready to answer the same question if it turns it around and asks for your opinion.

Step 4: At the meeting: come well-dressed—not necessarily to impress him, but to make you feel more confident. We all feel more confident when we look our best. After the small talk has broken the tension, present your one-pager, starting with the agenda. If I were meeting with the CFO, I might tell him that I'm here to solicit his help because the project team is lacking expertise in this critical area. Your goal is to disarm him by putting him in a helpful versus challenging state of mind. This is a better strategy than going in and throwing around accounting terms you recently learned; he'll pounce on you for that. Keep your eye on the clock, and be sure to keep the meeting on schedule. There's no greater show of respect than respecting his time.

Step 5: Verbally summarize the meeting in bullet form. Something like: "Harry, if I understand you correctly, your three primary issues are: 1.) Making sure we base our analysis on reasonable and conservative assumptions; 2.) That the underlying technology has not been proven viable; and 3.) The fact that we don't have a representative from finance on the project team."

If this sounds like a lot of work, don't worry. After a while, you'll find this method of prepared interactions will become automatic. You'll find yourself making a mental agenda and small talk points before virtually every meeting. Incidentally, I learned this from a woman that used to work for me. I always admired her for being an excellent conversationalist. I always found her to be charming and witty and learned her secret by arriving ten minutes early for a lunch meeting. While coming up behind her at a restaurant table, an unintended glance revealed she was jotting down discussion points for our meeting.

The Obstructionist

He is the organization's Dr. No. He seems to exist for one reason: to make sure things don't happen. Of all the complaints I've had about my employees, the vast majority have come from when a highly motivated star comes up against The Obstructionist. These personality types mix like oil and water, with fireworks often the end result. You've got a clear vision in your mind of what needs to be done, and he's seemingly there as your biggest road block. He might work in another department or she could be the gatekeeper (a.k.a. assistant) to an executive you need to see. Your gut's telling you he's doing this to pluck your nerves, which makes you want to scream "get out of my way!"

What can you do to budge this beast? Start by understanding what's motivating him. The corporation is a place where its constituents are in a constant battle for relevance. On the day your company announces a layoff, more than likely the victims will be the least relevant people to the overall mission. Most of us wake up every morning motivated to enhance our relevance through outstanding performance. If you close the Clark account, fix the troubled PR strategy, or pull off a successful new store opening, you'll be more valuable to your company than the day before. In contrast, The Obstructionist accrues his relevance by reminding people every day that things don't happen without his affirmation. Often his measurement systems (how he gets an "A" with his boss) exacerbate the problem. What's good for him rarely relates positively with your request. Ideally, companies would weed these people out of the organization, although as you probably have already discovered, they seem to hang on forever.

I'm betting you can already see the negative cycle that occurs. He asserts his ability to block things from happening, and people become disgruntled and complain, thus giving him what he wants—the feeling of position, power and relevance—which makes people want to bitch even louder. What can you do to break the cycle? The good news is that this guy can often be won over, if you're willing to invest the time. Here are a few techniques you can try:

1. Don't confuse being right with winning.

Yes, you are right, and yes, he's holding the organization hostage. The problem is trying to prove this point will only move you farther from your ultimate goal. Above all, avoid conflict with this person—he wins if he gets you riled up. Keep your eye on your objective, which is to get what you need to succeed.

2. Understand and respect his measurement systems.

Most undesirable workplace cooperation usually comes as a result of conflicting measurement systems. If the sales organization is under tremendous pressure to increase monthly order volume but the accounting department is being pressured to reduce the level of receivables (money owed by customers), you end up with a classic conflict: you can't increase orders without increasing receivables. What happens? Arguments, conflict, and wasted energy. The first step in disarming a cross-organizational conflict is to understand the way the other guy is measured. If you knew that the accounting manager was on the receivables hot seat, you could suggest that you are willing to try and get your customer to pay in advance. Whether it works or not, you'll surely get points for showing empathy.

3. Give him what he wants.

The Obstructionist needs to feel relevant. If you walk up to the gatekeeper-minded administrative assistant and demand an appointment, you're likely to get a lot of static. If, on the other hand, you pay homage to the difficult job of managing such a busy executive's schedule, you'll probably get much further.

Mr. Ambition

If Mr. Ambition was a collegiate cheerleader, he'd dispense with standing on the next person's shoulders, choosing the underlying person's head as a higher platform. I once learned a lot about people and their ambitions during an interesting corporate training exercise. I was at a management off-site meeting that was facilitated by a professional negotiator. We played a simulation game of nuclear disarmament in which each team picked a few members to negotiate a disarmament strategy with the other side. The overall goal was to find a means for both parties to disarm themselves without exposing themselves to a strategic imbalance. As an interesting twist, either team could elect to preemptively "nuke" the other team in a game-ending maneuver. While it was entirely possible, and desirable, to end the game with a successful negotiated draw down, a surprising number of teams elected to nuke the other side. Instead of creating a win-win, where everyone in the game looked like good negotiators in front of our bosses, they went for the sure bet...at the expense of the others in the game. Afterwards, the meeting facilitator said this was a common outcome—win-lose versus the harder path to win-win.

The term "blind ambition" describes a person that is so focused on his goal that he can't see the harm he's causing others. The father who is a workaholic doesn't see the harm he's inflicting on his children. The argumentative and aggressive boss doesn't see the demoralized bodies that are left in the conference room after he exits. Mr. Ambition will take credit for other people's work, he'll maneuver behind your back and at your expense, and he'll try hard not to let the truth get in the way of his version of his accomplishments. He'll suck-up, embellish, or denigrate...anything to advance his primary cause (himself). Got one in your organization? What can you do, short of quitting? Here are three lines of defense:

Line one: It always seems like the people with the least need to defend themselves do it with the most aggression. It's as if one moment he's a promising executive and the next he's a reactionary teenager involved in a playground fight. Whether it's the superstar flying off the handle at the inane comment of an average performer in a meeting, or the V.P.'s heir apparent flaming someone in an email, it seems to happen with predictable regularity. The odd thing is, from the boss's perspective, it's just so unnecessary. Don't you think he knows that John's an ambitious dope, and do you really think he's not smart enough to know who's performing and not? The fact is, the greater threat to the "A" player isn't the mean-spirited tactic of the corporate sniper, but the risk that the top performer's reaction will cross the line. Your first line of defense against Mr. Ambition is to not let him get to you. There's a strong probability that your boss already knows what's really going on.

I once ran into this situation and handled it poorly. It wasn't until much later did I learn what I could have done better. I was working at a mid-sized company as the head of strategic planning, reporting to the CEO. My boss asked me to join a team of two others, with a mission of coming up with a strategy to address a new market opportunity. One of the people that he assigned to the team was a recent MBA grad from an Ivy League school. Not only would she always introduce herself as "the recent Wharton business school graduate," she had the irritating habit of citing business cases she had seen at business school. When we'd sit down for status meetings with the CEO, she'd dominate the conversation, making it sound like the collective work of the team was her original thought. Perhaps worse, she'd meet with the CEO when we weren't around and say things like: "I'm sorry, but Harry wants us to do things this way." Is your blood boiling yet? Mine sure was, and my behavior showed it. There was much friction between me and this woman, which often spilled out into the open when we were meeting with the CEO. We must have looked like a group of petty, sniping fools. It wasn't until some time later until I got a better perspective. In a chance meeting with the CEO (after he had departed the company), when we were discussing old times, he used her as example about how frustrating his former job was at times. Hmmm, I thought he loved what she was saying, and now he was telling me that she was an ambitious jerk? I should have given his management skills more credit.

Line two: Your second line of defense is to remove Mr. Ambition's blinders. In many cases, the guy is so driven that he hasn't stopped to notice the win-lose situation he's creating for his peers. If, for example, he's always anointing himself as the informal meeting leader when a boss isn't around, you might tell him that he should give others a chance to lead. When you tell him "This is really Jill's area of expertise, so let's ask her to lead this section," you might actually get a reasoned response.

Line three: Your third defense is to confront the issue in a constructive way. Rather than running to your boss and saying, "I can't stand working with Dave another minute—he's taking all the credit for my work," you might try a more collaborative approach with the boss. You might say, "I need some pointers on how to best mesh my skills and capabilities with Dave's. I want to make sure you're getting the combined best from both of us." If your boss is on to Dave's ambitious tactics, he'll most likely relieve your stress by coming clean.

Corporate Politics

Oftentimes, the majority of the blame placed on corporate politics is overstated. Whether used as a convenient excuse by a recently laid-off executive or by a manager passed over for promotion, it seems like an overused scapegoat. When Andrew says, "she had it 'in' for me," in reality he probably had it coming to him—for the three consecutive quarters of lack-luster performance or the vacation he took during the last week of a make-it-or-break-it quarter. Are there political forces at work in just about every organization? Absolutely. Politics begin when you add the third person to a group.

The best weapon in the game of corporate politics is excellent performance. While being an alumna of the same college as the department V.P. might be of help someday, it won't matter if you're simply an average performer. High performance makes things harder for your detractors and serves to align your superiors on your side of the ledger. Average performance makes you prey as the corporate wildebeest.

When choosing your corporate politics, it's important to anchor yourself one level above the fray, preferring instead to let your performance and output speak for itself. Let's use the example of corporate rumor mongering. In most organizations it's become sport to pass along the latest gossip. "Impending layoffs," "the boss is in trouble," or "the quarter is coming up soft," etc. In almost all cases, you're better served not knowing about the information than being a participant in the rumor network. Hark, layoffs are coming! Well, unless you are skilled enough to hack into the company's computer systems and rewrite your last performance evaluation, whatever is going to happen is probably already set. Having advance information only increases the risk you'll waste time worrying or pre-reacting to the news.

The same goes for back stabbing. The people who talk about others behind their backs are verbalizing their insecurities. If I'm a "B" player, then perhaps I can make being a "B" player not so bad by demonstrating Joe is a "C" player. Resolve yourself to keep your feelings about your workmates to yourself. While you might feel like Henry is a jerk, you, he, or your correspondent won't be served by repeating it in public. On the other hand, if Henry the jerk ends up being your boss, you might not want to have been on the record as one of his spoilers—particularly if your correspondent ends up being Henry's lieutenant. You can think of this noise as nervous chatter emanating from the insecure layers within the organization. The perpetually average performer is like a gazelle on Africa's Serengeti plains. He spends his entire existence fearful of his day of reckoning with the unseen predator. How can you recognize these people? They're the ones who have time for rumors, back stabbing, and corporate intrigue games.

Speak out or Toe the Line?

It's important to remember that loyalty is a key currency within the corporate system. The concept of a company is to harness the collective brain power and energies of the masses, creating an entity stronger than the sum of its parts. Without loyalty, this system could not function. With this said, there is still plenty of room for individualism, whether in the form of actions or opinions—as long as you understand that there comes a time when you need to toe the line with everyone else.

Most good companies value alternate viewpoints as well as abject loyalty because both are important ingredients to a functional company. Let's say you are in a meeting with the aim of picking one of three possible strategies for your company. The debate is hot and heavy, with the participants lined up behind their favorite choice. If I'm the boss at this meeting, I'd be thankful for this level of passion and debate. I want to hear differing and conflicting viewpoints, but I'll also be equally thankful to know that once we or I make the choice, I can count on everyone to line up 100 percent, without reservations, behind the selected strategy. Does this make you a yes-man if you are required to line up behind your least favorite choice (the one you said you hated!)? Of course not. Rather, it shows you have the maturity to know there's a time for debate and a time for loyalty. I can also assure you that, as a manager, nothing engenders more confidence or competence than watching someone turn in an "A" performance without "I told you so's" on a project that they were against. It says: "Bob is going to make an excellent executive someday, since he clearly understands the importance of putting your opinions aside for the common good."

I hope you see by now that your performance is the ultimate arbiter in the game of corporate combat. The star softball player doesn't need to suck up to the coach, and the gracious and respectful tennis star tends to get more line calls in her favor than the persistent whiner. Results speak for themselves.

Don't be a Crab

I live in the state of Maryland, which is known for its Chesapeake Bay crabs. Marylanders eat them all summer, often catching them and eating them the same day. If you like spicy foods and beer, it's your kind of meal. A local waterman once gave me a lesson in crabs, and life, that I would like to share with you. When the crab traps are pulled out of the water, the crabs are typically dumped into a bushel basket sitting on the dock. They come out of the water with claws and fins looking to snap anything within reach. Curiously, most bushel baskets don't have lids. Now, the crabs are perfectly capable of climbing out of the lidless basket, although very few ever make a successful escape. Care to guess why they don't? Quite simply, when one crab tries to climb out, another one at the bottom of the basket reaches up and pulls the escaping crab down, in an effort to pull himself out. Sound familiar?

The crab basket is a good metaphor for life in the workplace. People often try to make themselves look or feel better by pulling others down below them. Mean-spirited rumor mongering and talking behind backs is the personification of this insecure behavior. If all the crabs worked as "A" team, they'd all succeed in their escape. Occasionally we need to shake a crab off our leg, and we often need to make sure we're not the crab at the bottom of the bushel.

Chapter 10

Learning by Observation

You can observe a lot just by watching.

—*Yogi Berra (b. 1925), U.S. baseball player, manager, and coach*

Progressing across and up your pyramid will require the acquisition of two distinct classes of skills. So far we've been talking about vocational skills, which you learn primarily through immersion in a job. Whether it's learning to price a product, register a trademark, dispatch a service technician, or prepare a legal brief, these are skills that you pretty much have to learn by doing. The second class of skills, often called "soft skills," comprises those that you most often pick up by corporate osmosis, meaning they're mostly learned by observing someone else. They are those important human interaction skills that do much to shape how you are perceived by others.

Soft Skills

So what are these soft skills that become increasingly important as your career progresses? Leadership is one such skill. The entry-level computer programmer need not excel at motivating people to take on difficult assignments, although the chief technology officer wouldn't be in this position unless he learned these skills along the way. Other examples of soft skills include interviewing and hiring, firing, employee coaching, customer interactions, handling legal issues, and dealing with outside stakeholders, like vendors, investors, and business partners.

You should remain mindful of how you want to fill each block of your pyramid with the skills and experiences you'll acquire while doing that job. If you're like most of us, your first few rows of blocks will contain mostly vocational skills, because in the early going, most of us need to focus on learning the basics of our profession. Over time, you'll notice that the higher you go, the greater your need for soft skills. In other words, your first row of pyramid blocks might be 80 percent vocational and 20 percent soft skills, but this ratio will probably invert by the time you reach the third row of your pyramid.

The next time you find yourself wondering how Susan has come so far in her career at such a young age or why Pete seems to be the fair-haired favorite of upper management, stop and take notice. There's a good chance you'll observe that these corporate fast-trackers possess advanced soft skills. Nothing breeds confidence within upper management like a young person who can nail a public speech, dazzle in front of a customer, or exhibit inspired leadership during a rough patch.

How can you acquire these important soft skills? Is there a way to acquire them faster than the ten- to twenty-year process? A key element of the human learning process is the way we learn through observation. From the time we are infants, we're subconsciously observing others and incorporating their social traits into our daily repertoire. It starts with our speech, gestures, and expressions, and it's later followed with the development of our habits, style, and personality attributes. (It's no wonder parents of teenagers find themselves saying "like" and "so," no matter how hard they try to stop!) In this chapter, we'll focus on some concrete ways in which you can fast-track the development of your soft skills, which are often more difficult to learn than the hard skills.

Plan A: Mentors

Before you get down on yourself for lacking a certain set of soft skills, it's important to recognize that it's impossible to be naturally great at everything—but almost always possible to strengthen a weak area. Virtually every person on the planet has a bell curve of strengths and weaknesses. Today's super-parent often finds the standardized testing process used by grade schools frustrating, as they expected their children to score high in every area. In reality, when you talk to the experts in the education field you realize that it's impossible to score high everywhere. People just aren't made that way. The brilliant mathematician might be weak in word association or the artistic prodigy might have difficulty with mechanical concepts.

However, our ability to learn from others, which began in infancy, will serve us well in the soft skills development area. One way you can observe and build these skills is to adopt a mentor or role model. Quite simply, who is better positioned to teach or demonstrate an important soft skill than someone who already has it mastered? Ideally, everyone's Plan A should be to have a benevolent mentor, always there to guide us along.

Here are a few rules of the road for selecting the right mentor and making the relationship work:

1. Win-Win

Virtually all business relationships must be based on a win-win premise. Even the most benevolent person will quickly tire of a relationship that is all give and no receive. So what do you have to give to your mentor? I'd start with the satisfaction of seeing you act on her advice. For a high-output person, the only thing worse than sitting through a long meeting with a wayward soul is seeing this lost soul fail to execute on your advice.

2. Good Observation Post

Your mentor should be someone who can routinely see you in your day-to-day career pursuits. While your uncle or neighbor might be a corporate titan, it's unlikely he'll be able to give you meaningful career coaching if he can't observe you in action. Your ideal mentor is someone who can answer questions like: What skills am I lacking? Where should I focus my self-improvement efforts? Or what should be my next move within the company?

3. Unrestrained Feedback

The ideal mentor is someone who is free to give you honest and straightforward advice and feedback. While your boss's boss might be someone you respect tremendously, chain-of-command issues will prevent her from being the mentor you want. For example, you probably wouldn't want to discuss a failing project with your boss's boss, nor would you be able to speak freely about a job offer you've received from outside the company.

4. Honest and Direct

The ideal mentor is someone who is going to give you honest and unvarnished feedback. While we can seek out praise and adoration from our family and loved ones, an integral part of the career growth and advancement process is having our insufficiencies pointed out. The ideal mentor is someone who is going to be both your biggest advocate and your toughest critic. Many people, including successful executives, have difficulty giving direct criticism, preferring sugar-coated admonitions instead—stay away from mentors of this ilk. Much like our ski instructor in Chapter 5, you want a mentor who is going to hit you between the eyes with blunt, actionable feedback.

5. Respect

Chances are, the kind of person you want for a mentor is the person with the least amount of time to give. Successful people have precious few minutes to spare, as they cram as much output as possible into each and every day. No matter how you skin it, slowing down to discuss your personal career issues isn't going to contribute to her productivity. I once mentored someone who was a master of finding "no cost" time in my schedule. More than once he drove with me to the airport or a meeting to bend my ear about an idea. He also knew that I was an early bird, so meeting for coffee at 7:00 a.m. was always a doable time. Making an appointment to see your mentor between his 9:00 a.m. crisis meeting and his 11:00 a.m. damage control session probably isn't going to get you very far.

6. Advance Thinking

A good mentor will expect *you* to do all the thinking. She doesn't want you to come and lay out your problems. She wants you to present the possible solutions. Instead of asking your mentor what your next career move should be, you'll be better served asking her advice on scenarios A, B, and C. Your mentor didn't sign up to be your surrogate brain. She expected to nudge and guide you towards possible outcomes. Keep in mind that your highly successful mentor is someone who spends nearly all of her time with other very resourceful people. Simply put, she's not used to people bringing problems without solutions.

The Mentor Myth

It's important to mention that most mentor/mentee relationships fail miserably in the early going. A meeting, two phone calls, a few unanswered emails, and the relationship dies a natural death. Sadly, most mentor relationships are terminal from the start since they are underpinned by a flawed set of expectations and unrealistic objectives.

You could spend all day searching online for a career book that *doesn't* say "seek out and acquire a mentor." *Thou shall have a mentor* reads the pedantic tone of the career author.

Similarly, nearly every career coach, vocational counselor, corporate trainer, and opinionated father says a mentor is a key ingredient for career success. It's enough to make you wonder why are all the experts telling us to do something that is almost assured to fail.

So what is it about these relationships that make them prone to failure? And what can we do to make a mentor relationship work? Let's start with the expectations issue. Here's the typical scenario: after five years in her industry, Anne has begun to wonder whether she is on-track and if it's a good time to make a career and job change. After reading a well-known career book and consulting her friends and advisors, she concludes that a mentor could help. What does Anne want from her mentor? Just a few unrealistic expectations: to tell her what to do next, make awesome introductions, give her key contacts, coach her through her personal issues, and be her biggest advocate and cheerleader. Oh, and let's not forget an important requirement. Anne doesn't really want to listen and act on the advice of her mentor. Instead, she wants the mentor to affirm the decisions she has already made. In essence, Anne wants a life coach that always telling her she's on-track. Now let's turn to the mentor. Here you have this high-output, successful person named Freda who has been approached by Anne, an aspiring but young career professional. When Freda first took Anne's call, she was intrigued by the idea of helping a young professional and, in her mind, she viewed it as an opportunity to give back. She envisioned an opportunity to craft Anne in her own successful image. In her haste to say yes, Freda momentarily forgot that her schedule is perpetually crammed and that finding time for bathroom breaks has become a real problem. She also neglected to consider that she isn't really in a position to observe Anne in her job, and chain-of-command issues will prevent her from being a sounding board for company-specific issues. Her first meeting with Anne reminded her how young workers can be, and she found it difficult to relate and bring herself down to Anne's level. She left the meeting feeling fairly certain that Anne wouldn't follow-up on her advice and was convinced that Anne appeared to be looking for a corporate godfather rather than truly investing in the long road of self-improvement. The dénouement was Anne's lack of follow-up, giving Freda the out, which condemned the relationship to the graveyard of right idea/bad execution relationships.

Plan B: Role Models

When you can't forge a meaningful and long-lasting mentor relationship, turn to Plan B: use role models as the next best thing. Think of it as your "best of" amalgamation.

There's a good chance that your workplace represents a good sampling ground for the range of human strengths. Among your coworkers and higher-ups, you'll probably find Fred, who is a great public speaker, Mary, who has a deft touch with clients, Tom, a born leader, and Harriet, the woman who doesn't seem to lose sleep when it comes to firing someone. While they might not be exceptionally well-rounded, they've come to excel in at least one identifiable soft skill area.

Assemble your best of collection of role models who demonstrate the soft skills necessitated by your pyramid.

Instead of trying to make yourself a clone of someone else—which we've all tried and failed to do at least once in our lives—try to clone a little piece of a larger cast of individuals. In many ways, this amalgamation mirrors the wish of most bosses: "If I could only combine Grant's enthusiasm with Meghan's customer skills…" While most of your peers are picking up soft skills through happenstance, you should try to make this an active process:

Step 1: Identify the soft skills required to build your pyramid.

Step 2: Identify the people around you who have mastered these skills.

Step 3: Actively engage in learning from these people.

A Word about Active Engagement

Identifying the skills you need to build your pyramid and the people who have demonstrated their mastery of these skills are the "easy" steps. The hard part is putting it into action. What does it mean to actively engage? It means to both observe and interact with these people.

Here's an example that will bring things into focus. I once had the good fortune to work for a company that was going through difficult times. I describe this as good fortune because it allowed me to acquire the necessary skills to lead through the inevitable down periods that every company experiences. During this rough patch, we went through a period of layoffs where for several quarters in a row we had to lay off the bottom ten percent of our organizations. I found this to be one of the hardest things I've ever had to do, and it resulted in many sleepless nights, stress-related health problems, and periods when I just wanted to quit. As I was going through this experience, I noticed that one of my peers, a manager in another department who was about ten years my senior, was being asked to make similar cuts. He seemed to deal much better with the stress and anxiety related to these difficult decisions and actions. If I was the clumsy emotional wreck, he was the confident and skilled organizational surgeon. I decided to ask him about his secret.

Our conversation went something like this: "Joe, you seem to be doing a much better job handling these layoffs. Why is it that I'm an emotional wreck, and you seem to be coping so well?" His response was very insightful. "Rob, I don't like firing people any more than the next person. But, in the end, I've come to the conclusion I'm probably doing the person a big favor. If I'm a good manager, by definition I've done a good job racking and stacking my people. When we're asked to trim our workforce, which is part of the management game, it really means that I have to lay off the weakest person. My experience has been that this person is usually someone who was bumping along at the bottom of the company, artificially propped up during the good times. Are we really doing this person a favor when we let him languish at the bottom? Chances are the person is miscast for the job—the root cause of most performance issues. When I send them home without a job, I believe I'm doing this person a big favor. I'm forcing him into an introspective process of self-assessment, which is a healthy undertaking for anyone who's performing below average. Maybe he'll decide to go back to school, become a policeman, or retrench—in the long run, he'll be better off from this difficult experience. Ten years down the road, he'll look at this as the kick in the ass he needed to make an important course change."

Joe's secret ultimately helped me install an important new soft skill area in one of my pyramid blocks.

Choosing Wisely

More than once I've seen people emulate destructive personality traits. Just because a certain manager's tyrannical methods seem to yield bottom-line results, it doesn't mean you should become a yeller and screamer. Aside from the risk that you can't carry it off, you'll most likely be escorted out with the manager for being one of his henchmen.

What's the trick for making good role model selections? The secret is external validation. Before signing someone on as a role model for a particular skill, seek out a second opinion. It might go something like this: "Boss, I feel I need to become better at interviewing and selection. Beside yourself (smile), who would you say is the best interviewer at this location?" Or, among all the managers in the area, who is the best at making good hires?

You'll find that with this focused approach, high-performance people will be much more willing to help you. If you ask a superstar to be your mentor, her first thought might be that she's too busy and that she doesn't know the first thing about being a mentor. On the other hand, if you approach her and say, "Tina, I've been asking around and I've heard you are the company's best negotiator. I'm trying to grow in this area; is there a chance you might be able to sit down with me for an hour and give me some pointers?" If she's like most people, she'll jump at the chance to show her stuff.

Keep Your Eye on the Objective

Your overarching objective is to grow and develop. You should do more listening than talking and never put yourself on the defensive. Nothing will drive a mentor or role model away faster than a defensive or insecure person. Your human development support team needs to feel that you are worthy of the substantial time investment you represent.

Over time you will find that you will be subconsciously drawn to successful people who can help you grow and develop. Once you train your mind to think in terms of self-development, you'll find yourself noticing effective hand gestures by excellent public speakers, motivation tactics of inspiring leaders, and the customer charming techniques of a polished executive. You'll develop into a better person by becoming more sensitized to the mastery of others around you.

Chapter 11

Resourceful Problem Solving

Obstacles don't have to stop you.
If you run into a wall, don't turn around and give up.
Figure out how to climb it, go through it, or work around it.

—*Michael Jordan (b. 1963), U.S. basketball player*

There used to be a show on television named *MacGyver*, which was about a government agent named Mac who could get himself out of almost any jam through ingenuity and improvisation. Think James Bond, only replace Agent Q's high-tech gadgets with duct tape and a Swiss army knife. He would invent tools, weapons, and electronic devices from household materials. One of my favorites was when he made a sonar device out of his stereo speakers to find a hidden door.

There's a little bit of MacGyver in most people who bring their "A" game to work. *They use their creativity and resourcefulness to find solutions to seemingly intractable problems.* What a psychologist might refer to as obsessive, I'd call determination to make their efforts fruitful and yield a solution. Whether it's gnawing on the problem all night in their semi-sleep or in the shower before work, these people obsess on finding solutions to problems. They're happiest when they've been given something that stumped the last team. Show me a resourceful problem solver and I'll show you someone who is valued by his company. A business is really just a problem-solving machine; it invents and delivers products and services that respond to the problems of its customers. By definition, it needs resourceful problem solvers to help it achieve its mission.

What's driving the "A" player's resourcefulness? It's a mix of commitment and initiative. It drives them nuts to have an unsolved problem within their realm. I always marvel at the clock-punching guy who doesn't commit his brainpower to the company as he drives away in his car with the $2,000 stereo system. Clearly that system took some serious mental energy to select, purchase, and install. It's a shame his company doesn't get a few of those brain cells. Being resourceful is about pipelining your mind with all of the tools and information you can muster—and letting it help you find a solution. When everyone else is saying "we're screwed," these people are saying "there must be a way." Their determination and optimism is infectious and serves them well when they enter management positions that require them to drive a team towards a challenging goal.

What does it look like to a manager when someone is lacking in this skills area? It looks like the norm as the vast majority of employees are hopelessly weak in this area. When Joe Average sees a problem or hits an obstacle, he dutifully abdicates by passing the news on to his boss. You can count on him not to spend a lot of time thinking up solutions. When he sees customers consistently returning a product, he rationalizes that he's just the customer service guy; it's someone else's job to fix the product. And when he presents solutions to a problem, he views his job as the messenger, never wanting to take a strong advocacy position about a particular solution path. To the boss, this passing the buck feels like he's pushing the risk on him rather than him taking a calculated risk himself. He sits in stark contrast to the "A" player, who always seems to have creative solutions to problems. Not only is the top performer willing to take a stand, he's also courageous enough to put audacious solutions into the mix. Rather than suggesting incremental solutions to fixing a product, he'll offer that it might be expeditious to acquire the competitor outright. Or if a competitor's salesperson is wreaking havoc in a particular state, he'll suggest that it just might be cheaper to offer the guy a big salary to come join their team. When he presents his solutions, you get a strong sense that he's already put hours of thought and research into his work; thus, as a boss there's no motivation to second guess his output.

Becoming a Resourceful Problem Solver

What can you do to improve your resourcefulness? Start with the willingness to be a problem owner. Your boss will sleep much better at night knowing that you're willing to commit your entire professional being to solving the problem. Tell him something like: "The account conversion process is off-track. I've been working on a remediation plan that I'd like to share with you next Monday." This approach is a far cry from the approach taken by Joe Average; he'd go looking for help with the account, expecting the boss to have all the answers. Here are some additional tips to help you become a better problem solver:

1. Bound the problem.

Before you can solve a problem, you have to know how big it is. One common mistake is when people underestimate the size of the problem they are dealing with; thus, spending time on a solution that will be too little, too late. If the product isn't selling, dredge beyond the surface level data to get to the true causality. If a project is off-track, don't just focus on the symptoms; dig deep into the causes of the project's problems. The last thing you want to happen is to have the situation deteriorate further as you are implementing your fix. When you're faced with a difficult problem ask yourself this question: "Am I looking at a symptom or a cause?" The skilled problem solver is like an expert surgeon; he doesn't want to operate on your stomach because you have pain, he wants to determine if it's your appendix or liver that is causing the problem. You'll get a few points from your boss for handling symptoms, and a gold star for finding and addressing the root cause.

2. Refuse the impulse to find a quick solution, which is almost always the wrong answer.

Tell yourself you need a Plan A, Plan B, and Plan C. We're all guilty of latching on to the first plausible answer, although it often leads to sub-optimal outcomes. The best answers are usually teased out of your brain, benefiting from having been slept-on and contemplated, and can stand up to the test of five other viable ideas.

3. Force yourself to consider audacious solutions.

You may want to ask yourself: if we had no constraints to our resources, we would do *what* to solve this problem the right way? Sometimes, the big, audacious solutions can lead to the best outcomes. Aside from the breakthrough thinking they represent, they also tend to captivate the interest of the senior management guys. While the rest of us are focusing our energies in the corporate weeds, they're playing industry chess.

4. Don't look back.

You've probably heard the term "buyer's remorse," which describes that next day feeling that says perhaps you could have gotten a better deal if you'd shopped around some more. This is a natural human emotion; we don't just want the deal to be great, we want it to be perfect, which leads us to look back over our shoulders. While we felt like we were getting a good deal on a car, when we wake up the next morning we want to revisit the purchase in an effort to make it more perfect. (It's also why we check the prices of products after we bought them.) The truth is, the game of life doesn't come with a do-over button. Second guessing yourself is an exercise in wasted energy and mental gymnastics. The better attitude is to say: "I'm going to fix this problem today, and if it's not perfect, I'll come back and attack it again later."

I once had a boss who, when we were faced with a seemingly intractable problem, used to say, "Time to start spending money." His philosophy was that very few problems in business can't be solved with money, so in theory, if you started spending, you were taking a step in the right direction. While you can't always buy yourself out of every situation, it can be very helpful to estimate the worst case scenario if you had to spend your way out of a problem. More than once I've seen an organization wrapped around the axel over a problem customer who proved that he was impossible to please. These customers can often force you to expend far more money resolving their problem than you actually received for the sale. Sometimes it's better to say, "We're going to spend $50K servicing this $30K account. Let's start the process by offering to give the customer his money back."

Early in my career as a computer salesman, I was involved in a very large deal, valued at more than $100 million, that came down to a brutal price negotiation. I was at a high enough level to discount the products on my own, but I had to get special price authorization from many decision makers in my company. The process was wearing me down, with a feeling that my credibility was on the line if the customer ultimately didn't buy. During the final stages of the deal, a senior executive from my company was visiting our sales office and inquired about how the deal was going. This was a high-profile deal that was on his radar screen. I told him that my insider at the account told me that our price was still $4 million too high and that they were leaning towards the competitor for price reasons. Thinking I was about to get a dose of sympathy, I was surprised when he said: "That's it? Call the customer and tell him we'll be down to see him this afternoon with a check for $4 million. Go ahead and call him—let's get this done today. We'll need to go to the bank first and get a check; tell him we'll be there after 12:00. " While I was down in the weeds, he correctly observed that this was only about money—something we had plenty of.

Proven Methods for Solving the Tough Ones

When you're faced with what seems like an intractable problem, looking outside can often help find a solution. Sometimes these external influences produce an answer, and other times they expose you to a new thought process or perspective. Here are a few particularly helpful avenues of outside help:

1. Seek help from friends.

Tapping a friend for help is admittedly the oldest trick in the book. I've found that my closest friends can be of great help, partly because they are very aware of my strengths and weakness. I'm an eternal optimist, and I often need a friend who knows I'm seeing the glass too half-full to bring me back to Earth to find a more realistic solution. I look at my pool of friends and colleagues as a type of cabinet; each of them possesses certain strengths that I can occasionally call on when I'm stuck. When you're seeking help from a friend or colleague, try to avoid a common mistake that plagues most advice seekers. When you approach someone with a problem, the greatest show of respect you can provide is to hear them out—completely.

There's nothing more frustrating than having someone argue with the opinion they solicited. For a lot of people, the push and pull of defending their position provides a means for them to affirm their belief in a particular direction. Unfortunately, pushing and pulling with someone who is donating their time isn't going to endear yourself to him. Also, be generous with your appreciation; sending someone a thank you note that says "Your idea worked great"—or, even if it didn't work out so well, "Thank you for taking the time to let me bounce some ideas off you"—will make them inclined to return your call or email the next time.

2. Search for analogies.

When you're faced with a big problem, it's often helpful to find analogous problems and solutions that other people or companies have faced. In the nation's top business schools, this practice has become the standard method of teaching. The case method is one in which business students study problems or challenges that a company faced, the remediation steps that were taken, along with the outcomes of these historical precedents. One powerful benefit of this type of thinking is the ability to offer the analogous situation in the presentation of your solution by being able to say, "Boss, we looked at a similar situation when Clark Corp. was facing a similar crisis of confidence with its product, and we learned that their come clean and tell the truth approach was very effective with their customers."

I can think of one example when a company could have benefited from looking at an analogous situation at another company. In 1994, Intel had just shipped its first version of the Pentium chip, when it was soon discovered that there were minor flaws in the chip's design. Under certain circumstances, it was possible for the chip to compute the wrong answer for a mathematical task. When the story broke, the press had a field day talking about how a much ballyhooed product was producing bad computational results. Intel adopted an aggressive defense, explaining that the flaw would only show itself once in a few billion calculations, and that it was "normal" for chips to have minor irregularities. Intel has a strong history of engineering excellence; thus, they treated this problem as if people were questioning their collective corporate intelligence. The problem is that Intel lost sight of the fact that people used their product in critical environments, including life or death situations. A personal computer spitting out wrong answers in an air traffic control tower, a hospital emergency room, or NASA's reentry calculation could cost the lives of real people.

The analogy? In 1982, Johnson and Johnson's Tylenol product was found to be poisoned with cyanide, killing seven Chicago-area residents. A murderer had laced several bottles of Tylenol and placed them on drug store shelves. When the story broke, the company didn't know whether the source of the problem was in their factory, the delivery system, or the retail environment. Without skipping a beat, and with their CEO unreachable on a transpacific flight, the company initiated a complete recall of every bottle of Tylenol on every store shelf in the world. The company's mantra was "safety first," and there was never a question that they had to pull the product. The results for both companies? In the case of Intel, they faced several months of bad press, a damaged reputation, and ultimately had to offer exchanges to their customers. At Johnson and Johnson, their customers never questioned their commitment to safety and the sales of Tylenol never wavered following the recall.

Another great way to develop your resourceful problem solving abilities is to read accounts of how companies have solved difficult problems. How can you do this? Start by focusing on reading more analysis and less news. The business news machine is a PR-driven process, fraught with company spin. Each and every morning companies deliver press releases to the media, who then turn them into business news stories. The problem is that the reporters of this news are on short deadlines, because they don't want to get scooped, so they take the easy way out by paraphrasing the company spin and posting it on the Web as news. Think you'll learn much from this? Unlikely. A better bet is to read more in-depth analysis in magazines like *Forbes*, *Fortune*, or *Business Week*. While a Web article might tell you about a Coke product, a *Fortune* article will tell you about the depth of the problems in Coke's soft drink business and the innovative approach they took to developing their new low-carb products. Don't be afraid to allow your brain to be exercised by the problems and solutions that are found in industries unrelated to yours. Often the best lessons are found in parallel events in different universes.

3. Tap into past discussions.

I often find the answers to my difficult problems are the identical problems being faced by others. How do I know this? I read a chronicle of their situation on the Internet. Before the World Wide Web existed, people used "usenet," which is a way for people to share knowledge. Usenet started out as a discussion forum for the scientific community and has morphed into a worldwide conversation between millions of people. Usenet still lives today, and can be accessed on Google's front page behind the groups link. The next time you're thinking about buying a new cell phone, try plugging the new model number into the groups search box. You may be surprised to find the thread from a vibrant conversation about the best and worst of the phone. If your car develops a strange noise, you'll probably find a past "conversation" about this very problem—as it was discussed by enthusiasts for this very model car. And, if your boss asks you to find the best meeting hotel in Dallas, you'll likely find a thread about this very topic. Wouldn't you want to learn from someone who has already been down this path? Building on the success of usenet, many people are writing blogs that accomplish the same objective.

Novel Approaches to Solving Difficult Problems

Solving problems is fundamentally a creative endeavor. The process of generating, evaluating, and implementing solutions to problems requires wide open thinking. When the airlines were all suffering under the costs of their expensive hub and spoke systems, which required travelers to pass through St. Louis whether they wanted to or not, a guy named Herb Kelleher at an unknown airline named Southwest had a better idea. What would happen if we only had direct flights on the most profitable routes? Every airline in the sky had the airplanes and gates, but none of them came up with the Southwest business idea. Today Southwest is the most profitable airline in the sky, while the others cycle through repeated bankruptcies. When Michael Dell started making computers in his dorm room, he rightly observed that people want to tailor their computers to their needs, and that selling through retail outlets would have required him to give 50 percent of his revenue to the retail store. His novel solution: build a factory that could build custom computers, all sold only over the phone. And when Bill Marriott Sr. saw his customers stopping by his coffee shop to buy sandwiches on their way to the airport across the street, he approached the airline about catering their flights. If you can train your mind to recognize problems and generate novel solutions, you'll be incredibly valuable in virtually every work context.

Defying conventional logic is what the resourceful problem solver does best. He's willing to put himself out there on a limb and offer up the solution that elicits an initial reaction from all that "It'll never work." Virtually every major corporate merger and nearly every high-flying start-up had its roots in someone standing up and declaring, "It's possible to defy the critics." When Larry Page and Sergey Brin started Google, it was when the Internet appeared to be collapsing under its own weight. The search engines were hit most hard, with Excite, Snap, and Infoseek being literally drummed out of the market. When they announced they were starting a new search company, it was if the entire world was saying, "That'll never work." Today Google is one of the most valued companies on the Internet. In my own experience starting CareerBuilder, I felt like there was a naysayer behind every door. I always tell my employees to move quickly once we find a great solution to a problem. Otherwise, the naysayers will catch up to us and doom the creative process.

I was fortunate to have a business school professor who passed along a little wisdom to me. He told my class, "You don't you have a great idea until at least ten people tell you it's a bad one." His wisdom has proven right many times in my career.

The Profile of a Great Problem Solver

As a manager, there are stark contrasts between the people who can and can't. When I hand out assignments to my people (which is another way of describing opportunities to shine) my method for choosing the recipients is heavily weighted by my sense of their demonstrated skill in this area. Managers want their problem in the hands of their most resourceful person. What are the attributes of these go-to people? The great problem solvers all possess these traits:

• **Persistence**

In the problem-solving realm, this attribute matters most. Your manager wants to feel that you're not going to give up on a problem too soon. When faced with a problem, the "B" player comes to the manager the next day after the next day asking for help; the "A" player looks like he's losing sleep searching for an answer.

• **Optimism**

A problem resolution process needs optimism so that its participants remain convinced that they should stick with the process. If the team leader is ready to pitch it in, so too will everyone else. Conversely, the leader who is calming, optimistic, and unflappable engenders an infectious can-do spirit among everyone. Another benefit is that your manager will put more responsibility (that is, opportunities to shine) on your shoulders. If I feel like someone is exuding positive energy that they're close to solving a problem, I'm much less likely to want to involve myself. Isn't autonomy one of the greatest rewards a boss can give?

• **Feedback**

The best problem solvers understand the need to communicate to their stakeholders. A common mistake is to think you can take a problem and go into your cave with the idea of emerging with an answer in a few days. The trouble lies with the fact that managers have a bad habit of assuming what they can't see, isn't getting done.

The better approach is to set expectations, describe the process, and communicate progress. It might sound something like this: "I think we can get to an answer in seven to ten days. My plan is to form a fix-it team. We'll meet every day at 9:00 a.m. and 4:00 p.m., and I'll give you an update every other day until we find a solution." Think about what it feels like when your problem goes into a black hole.

If you send your car in for service and you keep hearing that it's not ready yet, you're likely to assume that they're working on someone else's car. On the other hand, if the dealer was sending you daily emails that said, "We're waiting for the XYZ part from Ford, we've escalated the issue with the parts manager, and we've authorized it to be Fed-Ex'ed at our cost," you'd feel like your problem was in good hands.

• **Giving kudos**

The most resourceful people aren't shy about attributing credit to others when they find the solution. While I might remember the name of the person who had the winning idea for only the next thirty minutes, I'll walk away with an indelible memory of the person who drove the successful process. An additional benefit of this form of corporate generosity is that people will go to great lengths to help you if you'll provide an environment where they can shine.

A key goal of your career development efforts should be for you to be perceived as a good and resourceful problem solver. You want your boss to have a deep-rooted conviction that says, "If I give this to him/her, I can count on a well thought-out solution to the problem." When there are ten seconds left on the clock and the basketball coach is in the huddle calling the buzzer beating play, he knows who he wants to have the ball. It might not be his most skilled shooter, but it's almost certainly someone who has proven he can handle the situation. This isn't a bad metaphor for the workplace. By proving that you can be resourceful in solving difficult problems, you'll be increasingly called on to work your magic.

Chapter 12

Making Sound Choices

The aim of life is self-development.
To realize one's nature perfectly—
that is what each of us is here for.

—*Oscar Wilde (1854-1900), Irish poet and dramatist*

If you take a step back from your skills pyramid, you'll observe that it's really an upside-down decision tree, which makes sense since at its core a career is really just a continuum of choices. Study business or technology? A career in pharmaceuticals or medicine? Accept this job or wait for a better one? Time to update your résumé or stay the course? Put them on notice that it's a promotion now or I'm outta here? Go back for a master's degree? Join the family business? Take time off to raise a family? Make good decisions and you might retire at fifty-five. Make bad ones, and you might some day find yourself needing part-time work to supplement your Social Security checks. It's no wonder stress-related drug sales exceed the GDP of a small country!

If there is one place where we can all improve, it's in the area of making good career-related decisions. Perhaps it's because they are so often life-changing or maybe it's because they are so personal in their effects, but the pressure of making a good decision often leads us to make a bad one. This chapter is designed to relieve some of that pressure by equipping you with the tools you need to make sound and thoughtful choices.

Tactical Career Decision-Making

When someone approaches me for a career coaching advice, it's often because he's stuck in the middle of a decision process. Given the potential magnitude of these life-affecting decisions, it's not surprising that we sometimes become apoplectic. In Chapter 1 we talked about your career pyramid and the need to have an overall plan to achieve your objectives. Now let's focus your attention on the choices and decisions that go into executing that plan. Specifically, let's talk about improving your odds by making good decisions when it comes to assembling your skills pyramid.

If you've watched the America's Cup sailing race on TV, you've seen that each yacht is crewed by a highly specialized team. Each crew member has a highly specific job for tasks like sail trimming, manning winches, and steering the boat. Perhaps the most important position on the boat is that of the tactician. The tactician is the person responsible for "calling the shots" that direct the crew's activities. The tactician might decide to change direction to take advantage of better winds, change sails to adapt to changing weather, or give the crew a rest on a particular leg of the race. The decisions the tactician makes ultimately determine the outcome of the race. What you need to do is develop a plan to become a better tactician for your career. We all know someone who seems to be effortlessly gliding up the corporate ladder. While it's tempting to attribute their success to exogenous factors, or even luck, the more likely truth is the person is adept at making great choices.

Tactical decisions are the career decisions that weigh heavy on our minds as they present themselves on a near continuous basis. They might involve changing companies, applying for a new position in your present company, or making a major adjustment to your pyramid. If your pyramid has ten blocks, this means you'll have at least ten major choices to make, along with countless others which will happen within the context of any one block. Much like the tactician on the racing yacht, your success will be determined by the quality of choices you make as you execute your career plan. You can be the most skilled person on the planet, but a few poor choices could contribute to you finishing well short of your goals.

Career achievers who consistently exhibit good tactical decision-making skills typically do three things well:

1. They plan two moves ahead.
2. They always have a Plan B.
3. They are willing to tolerate ambiguity.

Planning Two Moves Ahead

To be a good chess player, it's essential to plan a few moves ahead. Rather than viewing any potential move in isolation, a good player knows her next three moves and has contingency moves in mind based on the potential counter-moves of her opponent. Similarly, being a good tactician means planning two or three moves ahead on your career chessboard. You may have heard that law schools teach lawyers to never ask a question for which they don't already know the answer. In a similar vein, you should never make a career move unless you already know the move you are going to make *after* the one under consideration. Far too often, people end up in a blind alley, necessitating significant career back-tracking just because they weren't thinking ahead.

Let's say you're in a public relations position and your boss approaches you about an opportunity in another department—one you hadn't ever considered. At first blush, his pitch is flattering: "We'd like you to consider taking the open supervisor's position in the graphic design department. It's a great chance to help your career and the company. This will give you a chance to develop your supervisory skills, and it will help the company turnaround a troubled department. With your energy and resourcefulness, it won't take long for you to have the department back on track." Should you take the job? My answer would be for you to refer back to your pyramid and answer the question: "If I take this job, what are my next two moves?" You might find that this job brands you in a way that would be harmful to your career progression. For example, if the top block in your pyramid says President of My Own PR Firm, this position might be of dubious value to your plan, leaving you branded as a graphics person two years downstream. On the other hand, if in the next level of your pyramid you have a block that says VP of Marketing, you might readily accept because this department head job would allow you to check off another key marketing skill area.

As discussed in Chapter 9, early in my career I was offered an international assignment that required moving to Europe for a few years. My friends and mentors all counseled against me taking the job, making me aware that international executives often get "stranded" overseas. The typical scenario goes like this: bright young executive-to-be is sent abroad for the "seasoning" that comes with being exposed to the international aspects of the business. While overseas, he's out of sight and out of mind of the domestic executive team. Next, the person who sent him overseas either leaves the company or gets promoted to another part of the business, thus leaving the expatriate executive "stranded" without an advocate to help him reenter the domestic operations. Does this scenario happen? You bet! In fact it's commonly thought that a significant percentage of expatriate employees switch companies upon returning to their home country.

After careful analysis and thought, I decided to take the job anyway, which turned out to be a great career move. In my case, I was not only prepared to leave the company at the end of the assignment, I was also convinced it was a step I needed to take. After ten years with a very large company, I thought learning about mid-sized companies would be an important next block in my skills pyramid on my way to being an entrepreneur. I was certain that I needed to move on and find a job with a smaller company; thus, the risk of being stranded wasn't relevant to me. The fact that I was going to do this with newfound international business and language skills seemed to make it a no-brainer move.

Over the course of your career you are going to receive many overtures to change jobs. When your friends leave your company, their natural course of action will be to try and encourage you to join them. (This is why companies have employee referral programs that pay cash if your friends join the firm.) While these overtures are often flattering, they should not be looked at as risk-free. A move like this one requires you to cash in your notoriety at your present company for being the new guy associated with the other new guy. Friends have a way of making these new opportunities sound exciting, perhaps to make them feel more secure with their own decision. How should you handle these overtures? With a dispassionate and objective decision process that answers the question about how it fits into the next few steps of your pyramid. If you think the new company can provide the next few moves, it might be a good fit. If it implies a major change to your career plan, or offers the risk of significant back-tracking, it probably isn't a good move. As a general rule, there's no need to make quick decisions in these situations. If the company is interested in you today, they'll almost certainly be interested in you tomorrow. So, take time to think about your best, long-term interests.

Having a Plan B

I once had a friend who was offered a terrific promotion with a successful company in a very small city in Colorado. My friend viewed it as an ideal job opportunity because it combined employment with a solid company in a location that offered a high standard of living due to low housing costs and exceptional schools. For the purpose of background, I'll mention that it was a marketing job in a defense company. Before taking the job, he called me and asked my opinion about whether he should accept the position. I had a strong sense that he and his wife had already mentally moved, meaning he was searching for affirmation rather than an honest opinion.

I had only one question for him: "What are you going to do next?" After letting him stammer around for a few moments, I pressed him by asking, "If this doesn't work out, what's your next move?" It soon became apparent that he had not considered what would happen if he were prematurely forced to make a job change. Perhaps he and the company would part ways because his style and the company's weren't a match or the company fell on hard times. What would he do then? It would have been nearly impossible to find another job of his specialty in that small market. Was he prepared to transplant his family again if things didn't work out or the company became troubled? In this context, he would be much better served in a geographic region with many more potential buyers for his valuable skills.

Knowing your next move includes having contingency plans. Good chess players are not only planning their next few moves, they're also planning their alternate tactics depending on the moves of their opponent. As you contemplate your next career moves, you too should always have Plan B alternatives mapped out as well. They answer the important question of "What happens if this job or company doesn't work out?" Incidentally, here's a tip that might serve your career-planning efforts well. Any time you find yourself using the word "hope" in a career context, a flashing red light should be blinking on your career dashboard. "Hope" is what you need when you didn't plan far enough ahead.

Tolerance for Ambiguity

Most of us fall into one of two decision-making types: those with and those without a high tolerance for ambiguity. It's easy to put a human in an uncomfortable state—just make their situation ambiguous. The time between receiving an unexpected note or voice mail from the boss that says "I need to see you A.S.A.P." and the actual encounter can be agonizingly ambiguous. Or how about when a company downsizing rumor ripples through the workforce? Having your tenure with the company suddenly become ambiguous is a recipe for more than a few sleepless nights.

The truth is, most of us fall into the ambiguity intolerance camp, meaning, we like our world to be rational and orderly. In career-related matters, it often leads us to make decisions too soon because we have a natural fear of putting our livelihood in an ambiguous state. In contrast, there's a high correlation between executive success and a high tolerance for ambiguity. The people who are willing to put off a decision until the last moment will often achieve a better outcome. Why? Because generally speaking, more time means you'll see more alternatives. If you allow yourself to wallow in the uncertainty of a decision process you'll often make out better in the end.

Here's a simple example: let's say you've decided to purchase a car and walk into a car dealership on the fifteenth of the month. Your present car is on its last legs, and you're worried that you're one commute away from another large repair bill. As you meet with the salesman, your inclination is to just do it and trade in your old car for the new one and fairly large monthly payment. The salesman proposes a price that seems in-line with the discounts you've seen on the Internet. Should you pull the trigger? Your first question to yourself should be: "Do I have to make this decision right now?" Sure, your old car might break down on the way home. On the other hand, a car dealer's sense of urgency tends to increase as the month wears on. Yes, the car might get sold later in the day, but conversely this dealer or another might get a new delivery tomorrow. Or maybe the manufacturer will announce a rebate tomorrow. If you're willing to fight the urge to make an impulsive decision, you'll probably make out better by keeping things ambiguous for a while longer. Waiting will possibly save you money in the end.

As the CEO of a company, I sometimes drive my staff crazy with my high tolerance for ambiguity. Often they think I'm procrastinating or waffling about something, when in reality I'm just letting things play themselves out so I see as many cards as possible. When they're finding it stressful to have a negotiation process lay fallow, I'm enjoying the opportunity to see if the guy on the other side is willing to show another card though his impatience. I don't doubt that we need to get this deal done, although I'm almost always skeptical that it needs to get done *today*.

Here's an example that might bring this into focus. Let's say that you arrive at work one day and are greeted by breaking news that your company is being acquired by a competitor. The competitor (a.k.a. The Evil Empire) is a notorious acquisitions company known for mass downsizings post acquisition. As you calmly make your way to the coffee pot, you see pockets of people with stressed faces, all holding hushed conversations. What do you do now?

If you're the typical low-tolerance-for-ambiguity type, you're probably feeling an intense need to declare a course of action. Perhaps that means telling your friends that you're going to spend the day updating your résumé or mentioning to your boss that you're not interested in working for the new company. You might even decide to spend the rest of the day surfing the job boards in an attempt to stay ahead of the anticipated mass exodus of coworkers. What's driving you to doing these declarative actions? Someone just made your tenure ambiguous! Put another way, your professional existence has just become uncertain. Your natural defense mechanism is to restore order as quickly as possible—even if it means declaring your new state of reality. The risk is that the actions you could take to make things less ambiguous could make things worse, not better.

Now let's replay the scenario by dialing in a healthy amount of tolerance for ambiguity. How would things be different? As you are greeted with the news, your first reaction is to say this is just one piece of data not yet worthy of a reaction. When you talk to your coworkers, you tell them that you're going to keep an open mind with the hope that a good opportunity might come out of the merger. You tell your boss that your mind is open and you'd like to hear much more about the rationale for the merger and what role might be available for you in the new company. You're open to taking headhunter calls and keeping an eye open for other opportunities, but you're not doing this in a public way, and you're certainly not doing it on company time. Yes, the situation is ambiguous, but no, making a premature declaration isn't going to make things better. In fact, it might shut-out an opportunity to add a skill in your pyramid—an opportunity offered by the new firm.

Make your decisions with as many cards turned over as possible. If delaying a decision will give you a chance to see more opportunities or have more data, then a slow approach might be the best course. This isn't procrastinating; rather it's making sure you are seeing the whole playing field.

Responses to Ambiguous Situations

Event	Low Tolerance	High Tolerance
1. Your favorite boss announces he's joining the competition.	When he asks, tell him you are interested in following him to the new company.	Wait until you see the new organization and meet the new boss before doing anything.
2. Your company inquires about your interest in a promotion but doesn't say anything for a few weeks.	Be a pest. Nag your boss. Send email and IM your friends.	Acknowledge that more may be happening than you know. Wait patiently, while focusing on doing your present job as well as possible.
3. You've been interviewing for a "pyramid maker" promotion, and the headhunter calls to say things look great for you.	Start focusing on the new opportunity, while losing focus on your present job. Take a day off during a critical time.	Realize that nothing is ever certain and that it's imperative that you keep the option of advancement with your present company open. Keep your head in the game.
4. Your company is being acquired, which causes the telephone to ring with headhunter calls.	Jump quickly to interview with a company that you have long admired.	Tell the callers that it will take 60-90 days to make a decision, leaving you an opportunity to see as many opportunities as possible, including with the acquirer of your firm.
5. Your company hits a rough spot, which might mean a downsizing or worse.	Declare your allegiance to the firm, assuring your boss that you're with him until the end.	Start the process of generating as many alternatives as possible. Be loyal to your company during the tough times but also create as many alternative opportunities as possible.

The Headhunter Call

Nothing engenders more of a sense of "I've arrived" than when you get your first call from a big-name headhunter. The message on your voice mail will often sound something like this: "Hi, Joe, I'm Jack Clark from Heidrick and Struggles. We've been retained by a Fortune 1000 company to recruit a new Vice President of Marketing, and I'd love to speak with you to see if you know anyone who might be a fit for the job." The obvious implication is that they'd like to speak with *you* about the job. This could be the sound of opportunity knocking at your door, or the start of a process that is going to whipsaw you.

Let's start with what's *really* going on here. A head-hunter's job isn't to hire the best candidate for the job. Rather, it's to serve up as many promising candidates as possible. It's the *employer's* job to actually make the hire. Start with the realization that you're going to be one of many candidates shown to his customer. Here are the ingredients of the headhunter whipsaw. You respectfully return the headhunter's call, informing him that you're happy in your present position but will give some thought to other people you know who might be interested. Of course he's paid not to take no for an answer, so he tells you that it's healthy to occasionally look at other opportunities. He also tells you that this would be a great opportunity to get placed in his company's executive database, which is composed of the best-of-the-best in executive talent. After having had a chance to rationalize the situation, you agree, and one of his assistants takes your personal information (so they can build a résumé) over the phone or via email. What happens next? He sends your résumé off to the employer, failing to explain that you're happy in your present job and that you took a whole lot of convincing to get to this step. Next, you get invited to interview with the company. Because you're a reluctant participant and you're not thinking they're interviewing you—rather they are going to try and woo you—you sit down to meet the company much less prepared than you'd be for a real interview. As they begin to interview you, you start to realize that the company doesn't know about your reluctance and is plowing ahead like you are an applicant for the job. The final step in the whipsaw is when you receive a rejection letter in the mail and that sinking feeling that you made a poor impression on an important employer in your industry. How can you work better with headhunters?

1. Never continue a conversation with a headhunter without his telling you the name of the employer. A headhunter will often be charged with hiding the employer's identity, although if you make it a condition of your interest they will almost always divulge the employer.

2. Don't buy into the b.s. that if you turn down a headhunter he won't ever call you again. In fact, the opposite will happen. Once they know you are an elusive and coveted target, they'll only want you more. A headhunter has tremendous respect for someone who shows loyalty to their present employer as opposed to the typically career mercenary attitude.

3. If the headhunter wants you to meet with the employer, insist on having a pre-meeting conversation with the employer. The typical scenario is for the headhunter to broker the meeting, which is generally a bad idea. A pre-interview conversation will give you a chance to tell the employer that you're happy in your present job and would need to be convinced of X, Y, and Z to make a move. This will put them in recruiting mode versus evaluating mode.

4. Understand that headhunters are experts at making bad positions sound great. This is what they do for a living. Most of their assignments have come about because the company wasn't able to find an internal or external candidate to fill the position. If your b.s. detector is going off when the headhunter calls, it's probably for good reason. Many of their assignments involve troubled situations or "mission impossible" assignments. In the end, don't let yourself get too excited or distracted as a result of a call from a headhunter.

Big Question #1: Should I Go Back to School?

As people are moving up and across their pyramids, there are two consistent questions that seem to make a normally decisive person a ball of stress. Often the root cause is that these decisions have a bigger emotional element than your day-to-day career decision. The first big question is whether you should go back to school for an additional degree. While MBA degrees tend to dominate the dialogue, sometimes it's someone contemplating a degree that would facilitate a career change. When someone asks this question, it really can be rephrased as: "Should I take the calculated risk of pursuing more education?" A calculated risk is one where you consider all of the possible outcomes and choose to expose yourself to the risk based on a set of sound reasoning. This is different from a blind risk in which you are exposing yourself to chance. In this case, aren't you really saying something like "Should I risk $50,000 and two years of free time to get an advanced degree?"

Start by looking at your pyramid and assessing the knowledge requirements presented by your overall plan. If you think you need more education to achieve your goals, then by all means incorporate that education into your goals and start saving your money. Where people often make a mistake is when they pursue advanced degrees purely for the optics—to dress up their résumés. This approach has things backwards since you get ahead in life by using your on and off the job education to help you demonstrate higher levels of competence in work assignments. Education should be used only to prepare you for future work assignments as opposed to window dressing on your résumé. The further you advance in your career, the more you will see that employers will weight your previous work performance increasingly higher than your education. While you may have been the sought after Duke grad when you were leaving school, your education probably isn't even discussed among the hiring managers for an interview that takes place at the ten-year mark of your career. Do the things that will allow you to demonstrate competency in increasingly challenging work experiences.

Big Question #2: Should I Change Companies?

It's a good thing to demonstrate stability and loyalty to employers. And it's a good thing to have been exposed to multiple company business processes, methods, and cultures. So then, how do you square these seemingly conflicting objectives?

A good rule of thumb is to stay with your present company if it provides a straightforward path to the next block in your pyramid. For example, let's say that you get a call one day from a recruiter about a Vice President of Marketing position at a mid-sized, family-run company across town. At first blush, the job is a perfect fit for you to fulfill the Product Marketing block in your pyramid. Should you go? Well, for it to be a good move it has fit within your overall pyramid. In this example, let's say your ultimate goal is to be a CEO of a sizable company. Perhaps the next row up in your pyramid there's a box that says Division General Manager, which would give you the "running a business" skills that will be invaluable to your CEO aspirations. Who's better positioned to give you this vital experience—your present multi-divisional company or the emerging start-up? If the family company doesn't have divisions, or they're occupied by the founder's sons, it could be fairly risky to take the position with the "hope" (remember, this is a bad word) that you'll be able to extract yourself someday and reinsert yourself into an environment which affords ample Division Manager opportunities. Unless the Top box in your pyramid says "VP in a Family Company," you'd be wise to pass on this opportunity.

Where Are You Going?

A substantial percentage of job changes come as a result of someone running *away* from versus *to* something. Perhaps it's because his boss is being tough on him, he doesn't see a clear promotion path, or it may be that he feels like he's in a rut. These changes often result in failed moves, jumping from one treadmill to the next. Why? In many cases, it's because the person hasn't faced up to a key personal growth issue (a.k.a. deficiency) that is holding him back. He thinks he can change companies in an effort to outmaneuver the deficiency, only to find that the new company eventually puts him in the same confining box—this time with less tenure. These people would be better served staying in place and facing up to their deficiencies instead of viewing a company change as the solution. More on getting stuck out of your rut to follow in Chapter 15: Going Nowhere Fast.

Personal Choices

Personal choices in the workplace are often the most vexing as they often touch our human emotional core. When we start mixing our business sense and emotional selves, we often experience, first-hand, the law of unattended consequences. At a minimum, it results in sleepless nights, and at its worst, it produces bad decisions. While most of us have trouble slipping into Robo-worker mode where we could make dispassionate choices, the reality is our human side often weighs heavy in our decision processes.

Example: Relocation Anxiety

Relocation issues seem to make most career achievers' top ten anxieties list. Over the years, I have seen people become wrapped around the proverbial axel about relocation. I've seen star performers turn down career-maker promotions because they didn't want to move. I've seen great people wedded to some of America's worst cities. I've seen excellent decision makers change their minds, and destroy their reputations, after they already sold their house and committed their company's relocation dollars. And, I've watched countless executives tear their families apart by trying to commute halfway across the country.

There's a bit of irony in this human decision-making hair-ball. Have you ever noticed that executives who get transferred seem to get transferred all the time? Keeping their addresses current in your address book is a real challenge! The common lore is their companies need their skills all over and must transfer them often to spread their capabilities. While it makes for a nice cocktail party story, I'll tell you a little secret: they like moving. I've observed first-hand that these people have learned to love moving. After successfully learning that they can break the bonds of home and stay emotionally intact, they learn that moving can be fun and exhilarating. It provides a chance to meet new people, see new things, and start fresh every few years.

Most of us have very strong emotional links to home, wherever that is. If you start the process of considering a geographic move with your emotions, you'll almost never make the "go" decision. Rather, your mantra *should* be to equally weigh your emotional and analytical sides in your business life. The frequent transferee demonstrates that emotional well-being comes as a desired byproduct of non-emotional decision-making and not the other way around.

You're human, and your emotions play a big role in defining who you are—whether it's avoiding the ego bruise that comes with taking a necessary step backward or making the difficult decision to staying home to care for a child. One helpful approach is to train yourself to equally weigh your emotional and analytical thought processes. Figuratively, if you were doing a Ben Franklin list, on one side of the paper you would have a column with the pros and cons with a pure analytical bent; in the other, you would include emotional factors in the column. It might look something like this:

Question: Should I give up my mid-level marketing position in order to take a backward step to learn more about sales?

Analytical	Emotional
+Fills a key open box in my pyramid	-People might think I got demoted
+All marketing people should be more knowledgeable about the sales area	-If I fail, I might be in no man's land
+New challenge	-I don't fit the sales stereotype
+Expand company knowledge	-Starting something new is always stressful
+Would position me well within marketing profession	-The VP of sales might not support me
-Less money initially	-I might be branded as a sales person
-I could fail at sales	
-More travel	
-Less visible position	

Conclusion: Take the job! The potential benefits to your pyramid far outweigh the potential downside risks.

Dispassionate, Not Passionate

There's often a need to mute your emotions from your career planning deliberations. In fact, I can tell you from personal experience that almost every time I let my emotions creep into my business life they had a harmful effect. You may love your boss, but don't let your emotional self stay with him longer than you should. It's a good thing to be exposed to many different leadership styles. You may love where you live, but you might be even happier in a new location with better long-term job prospects. You may be afraid that you might not be good at leading people, but there isn't a manager on the planet who wasn't apprehensive about her first management assignment. You could feel like you may be forgotten if you take an international assignment, or you could be one of a small universe of people with international skills. If you let your emotions rule the roost, they can lead you astray. There comes a time when your analysis and business sense all say "go." This is the time put your emotions in check and make an intellectually sound decision.

There's a funny thing about life. The bigger the decision, the smaller it seems to look downstream. Ask someone in his fifties about his first house purchase, and he'll tell you that signing the paper that said he owed $25,000 was the hardest decision he had ever made. Today he'll tell you he wished he had signed five more of those papers. With my most difficult career decisions, the word that most often comes to mind is "duh" (as in, how could I not have made that decision). There are very few decisions in life that are truly permanent. If you are going to make errors, err on the side of action.

Chapter 13

How to Be Happy...and Get Paid

To love what you do and feel that it matters—
how could anything be more fun?

—*Katharine Graham (1917-2001), U.S. owner
and publisher of news publications*

According to the Greek philosopher Aristotle, the core of human purpose is to seek happiness. We see evidence of this practice Monday through Friday when nearly every person we know expends inordinate dusk-to-dawn energy directed at this illusive ideal. We work for better pay, greater independence, a new car, or a college fund—all of which we believe will bring happiness to our lives. It's safe to say, very few people drive to work saying, "I do this to make myself miserable." We all want to love what we do and to reap the rewards that come from it. Much of this book has been focused on concrete aspects of your career and work life. *We'd be leaving out an important life skill if we didn't bring everything together with a plan to achieve the ultimate career goal: happiness.*

Before we begin the discussion on the topic of career happiness, we should probably discuss what it is not. It's one of life's great ironies that virtually all of us equate career happiness with financial success: *If I can just reach financial independence, a house with a pool, or simply $100,000 per year, I'll be truly happy.* Money serves as one of the few objective measures in the career progress realm; thus, it's easy to use it as a happiness altimeter as well. While many people have said they'd rather be rich and sad than poor and happy, there's very little data suggesting that financial success is the key to career and life happiness.

Economists and social psychologists have long known a truth that wealthy people almost universally discover over the course of their lives: rich people are no happier than the average person. Studies conducted by Ronald Inglehart, a well respected University of Michigan scholar, proved this fact by showing little or no correlation between happiness and income. His data suggests that people making $50,000 are about as happy as people making $100,000.

In the 1940s, two out of five American homes lacked a shower or bathtub, most were heated by a wood stove or coal furnace, and almost a third didn't yet have a running water toilet. During this time, real incomes (incomes adjusted for inflation) increased from $8,000 to $16,000 when expressed in 1957 dollars. So what happened to human happiness during this period? According to the University of Chicago's National Opinion Research Center, the overall number of people saying they were happy dropped noticeably. Incomes doubled, and happiness went down—interesting, to say the least! The rise of real incomes facilitated the purchases of clothes dryers, second cars, air conditioning, airline travel, microwave ovens, stereos, color televisions, and personal computers—all which were advertised as terrific life-enhancers—but somehow people were less happy with these and other modern conveniences. Let's not forget that during this period of explosive prosperity, we also created an entire new industry around the diagnosis and treatment of depression.

If you're not bummed out enough already, consider this: Britain's *New Scientist Magazine*, a highly respected European publication, recently published their World Values Study, a broad study on the relative happiness of people around the globe. Care to guess which nations had the happiest people? Would you believe the top three were Nigeria, Mexico, and Venezuela? Not only did the survey confirm that money can't buy happiness, it seemed to indicate that the desire for material goods can act like a happiness suppressant. In this study, the U.S. was sixteenth and Britain was twenty-fourth, which isn't so bad considering that a height-of-the-tech-boom 1998 London School of Economics study ranked U.S. happiness in forty-sixth place among developed countries.

Most of us can divide our daily life into thirds. We spend about a third of our time working, a third on life maintenance (shopping, eating, housekeeping, and leisure), and a third sleeping. It's safe to say that if you're dissatisfied with how you spend your working hours, it's very unlikely that high-quality leisure and sleep will put things into favorable balance. For most of us, when things are bad in the working third of our lives, our leisure and sleep thirds are somehow less enjoyable as well. Which is another way of saying that career happiness is an important element of overall life happiness.

Defining Career Happiness

In the 1990s Tamagotchi eggs were all the rage with kids. If you need a refresher, they were those egg-shaped toys equipped with a small LCD screen, a computer chip, and a battery. If your Tamagotchi was a virtual pet dog, you had to feed it, take it to the vet, walk it, and entertain it—and if you did a good job, it would be a happy dog, which translated to the game lasting for several weeks. If you missed a few care and feeding calls, the essential elements of your dog's happiness barometer, your dog died and the game was over. Now let's imagine that somewhere in a galaxy far, far away there are aliens playing with a Tamagotchi egg that contains a workplace human. What would they have to do to maintain a happy human worker who has a long life?

Before addressing this question, it's worthwhile to postulate that humans *need* to work. While the Romans believed the ultimate human achievement was attaining a life of leisure, this idea doesn't agree with our genetic code. We are programmed to be industrious, productive beings. This is evident in the incredible stories of people forced into survival mode after shipwrecks or other disasters. These survivors talk about the inordinate amount of time it took each day to gather food and provide shelter. It's well known that our cave-dwelling ancestors spent nearly all of their time on basic human sustenance. Unlike the feline, who is programmed to sleep eighteen hours a day with only brief interruptions spent expending explosive amounts of energy chasing food before going to sleep again, we're programmed to work from sun up to sundown chipping away at our existence. It's no wonder that modern man's waistline has grown in proportion to the availability of conveniences in our society.

Now back to our human worker in the alien's Tamagotchi egg. What are the key inputs you would need to add to your human's environment to ensure that he would have a long and happy career? If I were designing the game, I would include three special ingredients that I believe are essential to career happiness:

1. Active Learning Experiences
2. Positive Social Interactions
3. A Sense of Contribution

Let's examine each one of these ideas to understand how it will make our human worker happier.

Active Learning Experiences

Active learning experiences are those endeavors that are highly demanding and stretch us mentally and physically but in the end contribute to our growth as humans. In many cases, these experiences aren't necessarily described as pleasant while they're happening, but afterwards we can look back and say "That was fun, and I learned something." An analogy might be the rock climber dangling on the face of a sheer wall. While on the rocky face, it's unlikely that she's smiling and remarking how much fun she is having. More likely, she is saying, "What the hell am I doing up here?" But, after scaling the summit, her sense of accomplishment contributes to her inner happiness.

Mihaly Csikszentmihalyi (pronounced "chick-sent-me-high") is a professor of psychology and education at the University of Chicago. He's one of the world's foremost experts on human happiness and author of several books on the subject. His research identified a concept he aptly named "Flow," which describes the category of human activities that seem to contribute the most to long-term happiness. One description of Flow includes those activities that we enjoy that require a high degree of skill and commitment and that seem to make time accelerate. Often, the enjoyment doesn't come until after the experience when we can look back with pride and a sense of accomplishment. People can experience Flow while engaging in many high-skill/high-commitment endeavors including adventure travel, playing the violin, public speaking, pursuing a sale, debugging a critical program, or building a complex financial spreadsheet. The important thing to know is that these activities do more for your overall level of happiness than virtually any other endeavor. The research is compelling: the more Flow in a person's life, the higher his overall satisfaction and happiness with life.

It should be noted that there's also equally intriguing research suggesting that *passive* learning experiences do the opposite—they make us unhappy. Dr. Csikszentmihalyi's Experience Sampling Method research, which has been used on more than 800,000 people to measure relative happiness while engaging in various activities, showed that people are generally less happy when they are involved in passive learning experiences. For example, people watching television sitcoms were measured and found to be modestly depressed during the viewing experience. It seems that activities that contribute to long-term gratification, versus short-term momentary pleasure, contribute most to our lasting happiness state. It's because of this reason that mental health professionals typically recommend that a grieving person return back to work sooner than later. Why? Because we're more likely to achieve Flow at work than sitting around idle.

We would be wise to seek jobs that can provide Flow experiences. We should pursue jobs that are demanding and challenging and involve high-skill tasks and assignments that might not always produce moment-by-moment pleasure but almost certainly will engender a sense of pride and accomplishment. I don't know many people who truly enjoy public speaking, although I suspect it represents a Flow experience for the majority. Heading up a negotiating team, pitching a new client account, writing a new project plan, or handling a major customer satisfaction issue—they all may not seem like your idea of fun, but they might also be essential life happiness ingredients.

Positive Social Interactions

Our Tamagotchi human worker may derive a lot of happiness from the interactions he has with his colleagues and customers. Humans need positive social interactions. It's interesting to note that humans are Earth's only species with a true voice and a brain capable of processing advanced languages. It stands to reason that we somehow need these interactions as a form of cerebral nourishment to help us grow and develop. Before you say you and your dog have enlightened conversation, be assured I'm committed to sending apologies to all dogs that send me a well written email.

We all know that being involved in a verbally abusive work relationship can bring a lot of unhappiness to our lives. If you've received a flame email from a coworker or suffered a chewing out from a boss, you know how these interactions can drain your positive energy. Even if their arguments or accusations are false, they can gnaw away at you for days or weeks. In contrast, we're probably less cognizant of how positive social experiences contribute to our overall workplace happiness. A reporter once asked Bill Gates why he still worked after amassing his untold billions. His answer was telling: "I like hanging out and exchanging ideas with really smart people." Yes, he could be jetting around the globe in search of the best golf course or cruising the oceans in a luxury yacht, but instead, he prefers interacting on an intellectually stimulating level. Interesting.

The business magazine headlines in the 1980s predicted a rapid trend towards telecommuting. The articles predicted that our highways and commuting roads would become less crowded as workers could now take advantage of the burgeoning telecommunications infrastructure by working from home. Video conferencing and electronic whiteboards were going to create a "just like being there" experience. So what happened? Why are the roads still so crowded? Well, among other things, we learned that most telecommuters weren't happy with their situation. They found working alone to be depressing, because they missed the interactions with their coworkers. In fact, a few West coast psychologists coined the term "Telecommuters Syndrome" to describe the depressed state that can come from working in isolation.

What can you do to get more of this interaction-derived fuel? Choose your job assignments with an eye towards positions that will give you ample opportunity to have positive interactions. I'm not just saying choose a nice boss. Rather, look for environments that will provide stimulating interactions with others. If given the choice of working at Company A's headquarters or being a one-man outpost for Company B, you might find Company A will make you happier. While it's nice to like your coworkers and customers, it's even better if you can learn from them.

A Sense of Contribution

An essential ingredient of career happiness is the satisfaction one receives from contributing to a worthwhile mission or goal. When we drive home at night and reflect on our day's work, we want to feel like our contributions have made a difference to our company, industry, or society in general. This belief adds to our sense of self-worth and feeds our emotional core with positive energy.

I once worked for a company that was being acquired by a competitor, although the acquisition was held up for three months while the government investigated whether the merger represented an antitrust problem. The acquirer had signaled that they didn't want our employees to start new projects, preferring instead for everyone to just "stand down" and wait out the delay. The message was *just kick back, take it easy, and we'll call you after the lawyers figure this out.* For the first few weeks, most people took time off, went home early, or just went to the movies. Sounds like a worker's dream: goof off and get paid for it. You probably already know what happened next. Within a few weeks, most people were bored, discouraged, or depressed, because they no longer had that sense of contribution that comes from their work.

You might be tempted to say that your job is too far removed to give you the sense that you're contributing to the greater good. I once had an office manager working for me at a software company that could have easily formed this mindset. After all, managing the administrative aspects of the office is a long way from writing the code or selling the product. Some might even call it grunt work. But, contrary to expectations, Phyllis was one of the happiest, most positive people I've ever had the pleasure to work with. A chance interaction revealed her secret: she half-jokingly referred to herself as the company's CPO, short for "chief productivity officer." She explained that her job was to provide the necessary environment and tools so the company's programmers, salespeople, and accountants could be successful. Filling the refrigerator with sodas or stocking the supply shelves with paper and pens gave her the satisfaction that she was contributing to the overall mission of the company. You might think you're "just" the receptionist, or you could drive home every night knowing you are responsible for being the company's first voice to a new prospect.

It's easy to make a human worker unhappy: just take away their sense of contribution. The revolving door of people who enter and leave the U.S. government's technical projects is a prime example. The typical scenario goes like this: a promising young person works for years on an advanced defense project only to see the project cancelled by an incoming president's administration. Four years down the drain. Once he learns his job is about contributing to something that might never see the light of day, it's off to private industry. Similarly, there's substantial research suggesting lower career happiness among people employed in less virtuous industries, like tobacco. There's something in the human wiring that connects happiness with a sense of contribution to a cause or mission you feel is worthy; we should keep this in mind as we evaluate jobs and industries.

Personal Growth

If you were to encapsulate these three human happiness elements—active learning experiences, positive social interactions, and a sense of contribution—into one word, it would be *growth*.

Recognize that growth is not optional.

While we like to feel like we can define the rules of the work game, the reality is the job market defines them for us. Maintaining the status quo is a recipe for finding yourself on the wrong end of the diminishing returns curve. The military has long had a policy of "up or out" for its officers. When you are promoted to captain, you are also given a timeline by which you must achieve the next grade level or face forced retirement. While not a written rule in the civilian workforce, it's not a bad metaphor to keep in the backs of our minds. You need to force yourself to keep growing and to continue taking well calculated career risks up until your retirement party.

A friend of mine is fond of saying that people, like all organisms, are either growing or dying. Within this wisdom is the reality that there is no viable and sustainable state between the growing and dying processes. The course of our lives follows that of a parabolic arc, with each of us choosing the apogee on the arc's curve. While there are many examples of people growing well into their later years, there are also examples of people who stop growing; thus, they start dying at very young ages. The person who doesn't apply himself at school and follows graduation with a menial career choice starves his brain of these vital growth experiences and is actually living to die versus dying to live. Similarly, you are much more likely to die at age sixty-six than age seventy. Why? It seems the loss of a sense of contribution that comes with retirement often leads to acceleration of the dying process. I had a physics teacher in high school who was retiring at the end of my junior year. I vividly remember him telling the class that he recently purchased two ponies to keep on his farm. The reason? He said that without a job to come to every day that he needed a reason to get up every morning.

As we progress through adulthood, there's an increasing risk that we become growth adverse. While in school, we're all in the same boat because we're not supposed to already know the coursework. This creates a risk-free environment for learning. In our careers, growth experiences often require admitting we don't know how to do something or the expenditure of substantial energy seeking outside education. Sadly, most people develop a resistance to the learning process and consciously steer their career to safe, risk-free, endeavors. They might feel more secure. However, it's unlikely they'll find career happiness without these essential growth experiences.

The plight of the mid- to late-career professional illustrates this grow or die phenomenon. Take Joe, for instance. He's a forty-five-year-old engineering professional who is decidedly happy in his job. Because of outside interests and family obligations, he doesn't covet a demanding management position and has made a conscious decision to stay put with an eye on early retirement at age sixty. Leading people has always been an intimidating prospect for him, so he's consciously hovered in jobs just below the management layer. In his mind, it's "fifteen more years, and I'm home free." Unfortunately, Joe is headed for the midlife buzz saw. Let's take a look at the numbers.

Joe started the company with a $20,000 salary, which was the average starting salary for engineers twenty-four years ago. In his first ten years, he got raises averaging 8 percent per year, demonstrating his value to the company. Over the last fifteen years, he continued to receive raises, although they've ramped down from 8 percent to 4 percent, which means his recent raises just track the inflation rate. Even so, the laws of compounding make Joe's current salary $72,000. If he maintains a 3 percent raise for the remaining fifteen years of his career, he'll eventually be paid $112,000 per year at retirement. While this sounds good to Joe, it's also caught the attention of his bosses. Over time, his managers might come to realize that a young person fresh out of college brings new ideas, energies, and methods—at a fraction of Joe's salary. The recent grad isn't whining about being forced to adapt to new systems; she attacks them with relish.

So what happens to Joe? He finds himself out on the street with one of life's most intractable conundrums. He'll be overpaid and poorly equipped to compete against the available talent in the market. He won't be a candidate for management positions, because he doesn't have experience. And if he convinces himself to reduce his income expectations, he'll look like an even odder duck to potential employers. Would you hire someone who came in to your office after being out of work for a year offering to take a 50 percent pay cut?

Attitude Self-Maintenance

As a final point on attaining career happiness, pay special attention to giving yourself the mental care and feeding required to maintaining a positive mental attitude. Our subconscious mind plays a constant stream of messages into our psyche. Sometimes it tells us we did a great job or that our actions were virtuous and correct. Unfortunately, far too often it drags us down with concerns about our self-image, skills, or our deepest fears. If you take a moment and listen to that little voice in your head, you'll probably hear the words of your most critical detractor: *You can't do this. Why doesn't she like me? Jeff is so much smarter.* Nothing like having your own worst critic living inside your head!

I wish I could tell you why your mind feels the need to remind you of your insecurities every five minutes. Unfortunately, that's too far outside my realm; however, I've got a few tips on keeping your built-in critic in check. As you progress through your career, subconscious mind in tow, it's important to keep a few things in mind:

1. We're never as good or bad as we think we are.

Your professional emotions will often follow the path of a sine wave. You'll go through a constant cycle, where at times you'll think you are king of the office, and at others, you'll question whether you still have the right stuff. Everyone experiences these swings, from the office newbie to the star manager. You can take the greatest salesperson, someone who has made quota sixty consecutive months, and put her in a two month sales slump—and watch her question whether she still has what it takes. Ridiculous? You bet. Someone who should be brimming with the confidence of an experienced veteran is suddenly a ball of self-questioning nerves. You can take the PGA's best golfer, have him miss a few easy putts, and watch him begin a long career slide inspired by a crisis of confidence.

One of the keys to maintaining a healthy attitude is to keep things in the middle of the sine wave. You do this by reminding yourself that you're never as good or as bad as you think you are. By dampening the amplitude of your confidence swings, you can keep yourself in a more positive and realistic light.

2. Maintain a healthy definition of winning.

A key to having low workplace blood pressure is maintaining a healthy definition of winning. There's often a distinct difference between being right and winning, and you need to be mindful of these situations. We all know people who correct other's pronunciation of names or places, or those that argue about semantics or historical facts related to a project. While often these people are technically right, they are also wrong to unnecessarily delay a meeting whose outcome will not turn on the debated fact. Or, take the person who feels slighted and reacts with a burst or anger or show of ego. Yes, he has the right to defend himself, and yes he just "lost" by establishing himself as a hotheaded person. Similarly, sometimes it's better to share the credit with others, as the most direct path to winning a shared objective. For example, the manager could technically take credit for the success of the project in a review meeting with higher-ups. After all, the project was his idea, and his butt-kicking leadership made for a successful outcome. On the other hand, the smart manager might acknowledge that his primary objective is to advance to the next level of his pyramid, and being perceived as a great leader is more important to his overall career plan than being thought of as a tactical idea man. So instead of taking credit for the project's success, he chooses instead to explain it as a team effort, with him only taking credit for having had the wisdom to recruit, train, and coach a great team of people.

3. Live your life in chapters.

Rather than look at your life as one long epic story, it's healthier to see things as a series of chapters. With the epic story view, it's easy to find yourself feeling trapped in a bad situation, like a bad job or a troubled company. The situation itself isn't stressful, rather it's that terrible feeling that there's no way out or no end in sight. It's healthier to chop things up into chapters that correspond to your skills pyramid. If you happen to find yourself with a bad boss, a less-than-challenging assignment, or a company with poor prospects, you'll be able to say: "This chapter will be over before too long, but in the meantime there are things I need to learn while I am here." And, you'll be thankful you have a plan that puts everything into the big picture of what you're trying to accomplish. With this view, you'll also find that you'll start things with your mind in a much better place. For example, when starting a new position, you'll start with the mindset that this is only a one to two-year assignment, so you'd better go in learning as much as you can in those short months.

Over the course of this book we've discussed the ingredients of creating and executing a sound career plan. As you now know, a successful and happy career isn't something that happens to you, but rather something you create. You were born with incredible intellectual capacity, which you are free to deploy in anyway you choose, at whatever endeavors you believe are important. Your life's work truly is and will be *yours*. I'm tempted to wish you good luck in making these life-defining choices, but I recognize that luck is what you need when you don't have a plan.

Part Two

Emergency Procedures

What to Do When Things Aren't Going According to Plan

If everything seems under control,
you're just not going fast enough.

—*Mario Andretti (b. 1940), Italian-born, U.S. automobile racecar driver*

Chapter 14

Lost Your Job? Now What?

Business opportunities are like buses;
there's always another one coming.

—*Richard Branson (b. 1950), British entrepreneur
and founder of Virgin Enterprises*

In the summer of 1995, I was on top of the world. At only thirty-three-years-old, I was vice president and general manager of a $200 million division of the world's fourth-largest software company. I had left a great career at Hewlett-Packard to join Legent Corporation in order to fill out my skills pyramid with division operating experience, which I knew would be critical to my goal of being a start-up CEO. I had 300 employees, a big salary, a corner office in my own building, and enough perks to satisfy a foreign leader. Life was sweet.

Until I lost my job. I'll never forget that 10:30 a.m. call to my wife, telling her I was on my way home. What would I tell the rest of my family? What would my friends, most of whom had come to think of me as a super-achiever, think? What was

my next move? Legent was being acquired by Computer
Associates, the second-largest software company, and my pink
slip was evidence their management team would be taking
over "our" positions. In acquisition parlance, we were being
"consolidated." I was living and breathing proof of the bigger
they are, the harder they fall axiom.

Thankfully, the story had a positive ending. My prior
thirteen years of pyramid building had left me well-prepared
to weather a setback such as this one. I ultimately decided to
use this lay-off as an opportunity to strike out on my own and
start CareerBuilder. I learned a lot from this seemingly huge
career setback, as well as from being a principle actor in many
hirings, firings, layoffs, and consolidations. In this chapter I'd
like to share the fruits of the hard-earned lessons that have
come out of these experiences.

Stop Signs along the Road to Success

Setbacks are a part of life in today's workforce. There may be
no truer measure of the character of a person than how he
deals with career adversity. Are you the type to get angry?
Resentful? Remorseful? All are unhelpful emotions when
we're talking about careers. If there's one time when we need
to have the inner strength to dust ourselves off and reengage,
it's during these setbacks. When I read about successful
people, I'm often inspired to learn about the adversity they
faced. Lee Iaccoca, the CEO that saved the Chrysler
Corporation, was "available" for the Chrysler job for one
reason: he had just been fired by Ford Motor Company.
Before joining the New England Patriots, where he tied the

record for most Super Bowl wins, Bill Belichick was fired as the Cleveland Browns coach for having only one winning season during his five-year tenure. The first President Bush ran against Ronald Reagan and lost big in the primaries. And Steve Jobs, the CEO of both Apple and Pixar, was fired by Apple in 1984 before being asked to rejoin the company as a turnaround CEO in 1997. Somehow the world would be a less interesting place if anytime someone was fired he drifted off into the ether. Resilience is one of the most admirable attributes a person can possess.

Something in the Wind

The scene: your office, a typical Monday morning. You arrive at work like usual, and for some reason you can't log on to your email account. Or perhaps there's a see-me note from your boss. Or maybe you receive a memo saying there's an unscheduled, all-hands meeting in the main conference room. Or possibly you and your boss have been discovering that this job isn't a good fit for you and the move-up-or-out performance evaluation deadline has arrived.

Occasionally we get tipped off that we're about to lose our jobs. Sometimes it's a compassionate boss who says, "It's time to start looking," and other times it's just the writing on the wall. If your boss begins hinting around for you to polish up the old résumé, then that means get a move on it, fast.

Your odds of finding a good job while you're still employed are much greater than when you're not working. In fact, I'm hard-pressed to think of someone who took a lesser job while they were already employed. In contrast, I've known many people who spend six months looking for a job only to settle for a lower-paying, less interesting one. Many "A" players use a tactic that helps to insulate them from sudden unemployment. They strike an informal, verbal deal with their boss that says: "I'll give you at least a month's notice if I'm going to leave, if you'll give me the same courtesy."

But what about the difficult situation when you're going down with the ship? Perhaps your location is being closed or the business is in an unrecoverable dive. Remember, there isn't a Hall of Fame for Loyalty. Your loyalty commitment needs only extend to the point where your future livelihood is at risk. Often a company will offer a stay bonus for those employees who will ride out a major closing or a merger consolidation. If this happens to you, negotiate job search time along with any stay bonus offer. In other words, your offer should be: "I'll stay to the bitter end of the shutdown, although I need ten hours per week for job search and interview time."

Whether delivered personally or en masse, you've just learned that you and/or your coworkers will soon be scrambling for the office supplies on your desk. Whether you're faced with being downsized, laid off, or fired, let's discuss the steps you can take before, during, and after you're left without a job to minimize the potential for a major career setback.

So, You've Been Downsized/Laid Off/Fired

Wouldn't it be wonderful if assembling our pyramid blocks was a process of continuous upward building culminating in reaching the apex of our pyramid—our career goal? In reality, as we've discussed, the block building progress will have its share of ups and downs, making it more of a pyramid than a ladder to success. The downs often come as a byproduct of taking calculated risks, which are essential to career advancement. Maybe you're losing your job because you made a bet on a speculative company or perhaps it's because you were placed in a job that was too much, too soon. Or maybe your company has been acquired and is undergoing a major reshuffling. I have a friend who says if you aren't missing your flights once in a while, you're spending too much time in airports. The analogy fits here as well. If you aren't experiencing the occasional career setback, you're probably not pushing yourself far enough on the risk/reward continuum. It's not possible to grow without making mistakes and learning from them.

First, Do No Harm: The Anatomy of a Firing

In 400 B.C. a pioneering Greek physician named Hippocrates wrote what's now known as the Hippocratic Oath. To this day, the vast majority of medical school grads take this pledge before embarking on their careers, and it serves as a sort of ethical backbone for the medical profession. Within this pledge is the concept of "first, do no harm." In other words, physicians start their treatment efforts with the goal of not making things worse. There's a corollary here in the termination scenario: your first objective should be to do no harm. Above all else, you don't want to make an already difficult situation worse.

Before addressing the array of potentially harmful actions you could take, let's first dissect the anatomy of a firing, perhaps the scariest of all ways to lose your job. I'd like to start with the boss's perspective, because it often doesn't get the understanding that it deserves. No one likes to fire another human being. It's among the most gut-wrenching, agonizing, and hurtful acts a manager ever has to endure. No matter if it's your first or five hundredth time, taking away someone's livelihood does not get any easier. The night before he has to fire you, your boss probably has a sleepless night, nervous about confronting you and worried about your reaction. Perhaps he knows that you've given everything to this job and that you have little financial cushion to fall back on. As the clock ticks toward the meeting hour, he's wondering whether he can control his nerves enough to speak clearly and whether he'll emotionally fall apart right alongside of you.

Why the lecture on the executioner's plight? (Aside from exercising our Chapter 8 empathy skills?) Well, to start with, it raises the stakes in the "do no harm" area. For example, let's say that you're like most people and you react with anger and disbelief to the situation. I don't know about you but having an angry conversation with someone who hasn't slept or eaten in the past twenty-four hours isn't my idea of a picnic. Chances are, your anger will result in an escalation of the already palpable tension, and may lead to your boss thinking "Now I really know why I fired him!" It's safe to say that very few people have argued their way back to having a job once the boss shows them the door. *Instead, your sole objective should be to do no harm.* Do not leave your boss (and the company) with a negative impression of you.

Turn Your Firing into a Negotiation

You're about to redirect the discourse, from briskly showing you the door to extracting a few valuable concessions. For this to work, you need to remain calm and get your head around this new reality. An emotional show of anger or resentment will almost certainly doom this strategy. There's no emotional reaction that you can summon that will change the reality you are now facing. While it might not feel like it, you're still alive and you're still in control of your own destiny. After all, it's just a job. Remember, your boss is most likely feeling bad about letting you go. What can make him feel better? Knowing that he made things as comfortable as possible for you. *Therein lies your opportunity.* You can make your boss feel better, and he can make things more comfortable for you, which serves as the basis for a win-win negotiation that you're about to have. Here are a few rules to live by as you conduct this negotiation:

Rule #1: Make it quick.

This isn't a house purchase you can drag out over three weeks. Chances are if you're going to get the sweetener that you want, the negotiation has to come at, or within a few hours, of the firing.

Rule #2: Keep it reasonable.

If they're offering you four weeks of severance, don't counter by asking for a year with pay and benefits.

Rule #3: Be wary of your friends who practice law without a license.

One of the easiest things to do is give uninformed legal advice to someone based on sketchy knowledge.

Many a friend has said "they can't legally do that" upon hearing of a friend's termination, although very little of that "legal advice" proves accurate. In most all states the law is clear: a company is free to terminate an employee so long as the employer isn't discriminating. They can't fire you for being a certain color or a certain age, but otherwise everything else is fair game. If you don't "fit in" or they need to cut back on expenses or they don't like how you dress, it's their call. Never play a legal card unless you're fully prepared to see the matter through to litigation. Most law firms I know wouldn't take an employment matter on contingency, meaning you'll probably need $100,000 to play the legal card in this situation. This is partly because Rule #1 in the corporate lawyers' book of dealing with a disgruntled employee suits is "force him to spend money." Any delays will give you frighteningly large bills. Statistically speaking, employers win the vast majority of these legal skirmishes.

Rule #4: Know what you want ahead of time.

Ask yourself before you get the bad news: if I got fired tomorrow, what things would I want on my way out the door? Most people make the mistake of reverting to the primal by asking for more money. Not only is this request the hardest thing for the firing manager to produce, it might also be the least valuable concession you can extract. A good rule of thumb is to keep things in the decision realm of your boss's authority. Requesting the things he can grant right there at the table, without consulting his boss or the Human Resources Department, should be your objective.

So, what do you request? Think lifetime earnings potential. How about asking for a positive reference letter from your boss? This reference not only costs your boss nothing, but it could help you smooth over a résumé worry later. Asking to be kept on the payroll through your severance period is also a good tactic as it may alleviate you from a having to disclose that you're unemployed in your next interview. It could mean the difference between a great interview and one that goes flat under a cloud of suspicion. Perhaps the company will let you use your voice mail and email address during this time. It's also becoming common to ask, and have your request granted, to keep your laptop, cell phone, and Palm Pilot, all of which might be helpful in your upcoming job search process.

Keep in mind that the receipt of a "sweetener" will almost certainly require you to waive your future rights to seek legal recourse against the company. This is a reasonable position for the company to take, and most often, for you to accept.

Rule #5: Agree on the official reasoning for your dismissal.

Just because you're being terminated doesn't mean that's how it has to be portrayed to the world. If you're being let go in a mass layoff, you may not want to spend time wordsmithing this outcome. On the other hand, if you're being fired because you were a poor fit for the job, you might ask that it be recorded as you resigning instead. Most employers are willing to offer this face-saving gesture, mostly because it relieves them of the potential legal liability for a wrongful firing.

Just keep the following in mind as you contemplate your desired official reasoning:

1. In many states you are not eligible for unemployment benefits if you resign.

2. Resigning in lieu of being fired will almost certainly involve you waiving your rights to sue the company.

3. Over the years, the COBRA laws (they specify the conditions and duration of the medical benefits your employer must make available to you—at your cost—in the event of a termination) have vacillated on whether you deserve more or less protections if you are fired.

You've Turned in Your Company Badge—Now What?

You've got your box of personal effects in-hand and you're headed for your car. So, what's next? Round up some friends and drink away your sorrows at the local pub? Celebrate your "early release" from your job?

Your next steps are critical. One of the most common mistakes people make comes immediately after the termination. The shell-shocked person decides to take some time off, decompress, and perhaps take that long-postponed vacation to the islands. If he was granted eight weeks' severance, he rationalizes, "I'll take the first four weeks off, and then I'll start looking in the second four weeks." If you're someone with substantial financial means, call your travel agent and go for it. If, on the other hand, you've got less than one year's salary in the bank, focus on recovery first and time off second. Here's a five-step plan to guide your actions:

Step #1: Slow the cash burn.

Some people find a job in two weeks, and others take a year. Paring back your expenses will give you more time, and less stress, if it ends up that you're less marketable than you think. Generally speaking, the economy is a place where the game ends when you run out of cash.

Step #2: Address the two big benefits decisions: Medical and 401(K).

In most all cases, you are entitled to continue your medical benefits, at your own cost, and to rollover your 401(K) investments to either another qualifying 401(K) or to an IRA account. The laws that entitle you to these medical protection benefits are referred to as COBRA and are designed to ensure that a person isn't suddenly thrust into the world without the ability to secure medical insurance.

Step #3: Take deliberate action on starting a job search.

Don't be rash, but don't lollygag either. It's much more likely that you'll find a job within a few weeks of your separation from the previous company than a few months. The longer you're out of a job, the more questions an employer will have about you. Explaining that you've been in Tahiti and have been fulfilling your personal desire to learn native woodworking isn't likely to sway a hiring manager.

Step #4: Control the flow of information to your network.

It is better that your contacts hear the news from you than fourth-hand on the whisper down the lane circuit.

Step #5: Use outplacement services if they are offered.

In a large layoff scenario, many companies will offer the services of an outplacement firm to help people find a new job. There is a tendency to categorize these services as a feeble appendage of the former company, with most people declining to take advantage of this resource. Everyone I know who has ever used these services raves about them. Here's how it works. When a company is conducting a workforce reduction, it will often contract with an outplacement firm to provide assistance to the displaced people. Most of these firms are excellent at what they do—help laid off workers find a new job. And just to be clear, they charge the company conducting the workforce reduction on a per enrolled employee basis. You won't be charged for this help.

So, when can you take that trip to Bora Bora? After you've found your next job. It's far better to tell your new employer that you can start in fourteen days than to lose that jump in your job search process.

Before You Fill in Your Next Box on Your Skills Pyramid...

Your job hunt has begun in earnest. What can you do to improve your changes of landing a great job quickly? Where do you need to be heading to continue on your life skills path?

Bad Reference Prevention Strategies

One of the most stressful parts of the firing process involves the unknown: "What will my former employer say about me?" Or, "Will their silence hurt me?" It's well-known in Human Resources circles that a "no comment" or an unanswered reference request is translated into a negative opinion about the person. Don't be fooled by the large company policy of not providing references. Sure, the Human Resources Department might stick to that policy, although every line manager I know will provide a confidential reference for a good person. It's a generally understood truth that a no reference response to an inquiry to a candidate's former line manager is equivalent to a negative response. Hoping your company won't say anything negative about you might not be the most desirable outcome.

While one strategy is to move to the opposite coast and adopt a new identity, the better approach is to address the reference issue head-on. Fortunately, there are steps that you can take to improve your odds of receiving a better reference from your former employer. Here are a few tactics that you might want to consider:

Strategy #1: The pre-agreed reference letter.
We already discussed the possibility of asking your former employer for a letter of reference on your departure from the company. Generally speaking, these letters are easy to attain. There is another category of these letters that may surprise you. Are you aware that there are many people who are employed in good standing that already have a letter of reference written for them? How could that be, you may be wondering. Well, let's say your employer asks you to take a mission impossible kind of job. Perhaps it's to turn around a failing sales territory or to go to work within a division that's teetering toward disaster. If you're smart, you'd ask for the separation reference letter as a condition of accepting the risky position. Your request might go something like this: "Boss, I'm willing to take this difficult position although we both need to acknowledge the potential risk to my position. As a condition, I'd like to ask for a letter of reference that says I was an excellent employee at the risk that you or your successor needs to throw this baby out with the bath water."

Strategy #2: The employment post-mortem.
Conducting a post-mortem with your previous employer is a powerful way to head-off a negative reference. Here's the typical scenario that you can avoid. A manager fires Fred for poor performance. Perhaps Fred was having trouble getting his hands around the job or he was deficient in a few key skill

areas. Shortly after letting Fred go, the previous employer gets a call from a company across town wanting a reference for Fred for a similar position. Now the manager is irked, thinking "Why can't Fred face up to his faults?" and "I can't let this company make the same mistake." Don't be a deadhead Fred!

There is a better way. After the dust has cleared with your former employer, call your old boss and ask to take him to lunch for a post-mortem. During this meeting you want to be contrite and listen without saying one defensive word—even if he insults your mother. The meeting might start by you saying, "In spite of how things ended, I wanted you to know how much I enjoyed working for Acme Corp. and, specifically, how much I learned from you. As you know, I'm looking for a new job, and I was wondering if you would mind giving me a post-mortem on my employment with you? I'm committed to personal growth and want to make sure I incorporate your critical thoughts into my development plans. I also want to make sure not to make the same mistakes in the future." Jot down a few notes, probe him to be sure he's not holding back, thank him for his time, and don't forget to pick up the check. End the meeting by asking him whether he thinks you should use him as a reference—you'll probably be surprised by his answer.

Strategy #3: The advantage of searching for a job while you're still employed.

Earlier in this chapter we discussed how the smart person would prefer to have their severance paid out over time rather than taking a lump sum on departure, thus technically remaining on the payroll longer. The ability to say you're still employed has an added benefit—how many prospective employers do you think expect to call your present employer for a reference? If you answered zero, you're close.

The Reference Network: Above and Below the Board

It's important to remember there are really two levels to the reference network. There's the official network, which attempts to comply with corporate policy. Some of the more common policies you'll find are: a.) The company doesn't provide references; b.) All reference requests are made and answered in writing; or c.) All requests and responses must be channeled through the HR office. These and other policies are designed to protect a company from a disgruntled former employee suing because he believes they unfairly harmed his future earnings potential.

On another level is the shadowy below the surface reference network. This network is often held together by the linkages of friends and relationships. Sure, I might not get anywhere by calling a candidate's former employer's HR department, but calling a friend who works at the company is certain to get me the real scoop. This fact underlines the need to conduct your post-mortem as well as to take any and all steps to neutralize your prior employer's detractors.

Let's say you've done everything humanly possible to prevent a bad reference but your former boss is hell-bent on casting dispersions about you. Fortunately, this is a rare circumstance. The only reliable way to handle this situation is to hit the issue head-on with your prospective new employer. While not guaranteed to keep you in the job hunt, it's still better than someone finding a landmine during the reference checking process. It might go something like this: "I want you to know upfront that it wasn't my choice to leave Acme. My boss concluded that I'm really not cut out for a career in quantum mechanics, and I have to say after much consideration that I agree with him. My skills are more suited to chemical engineering, and my references would concur that it is my core strength area." Again, addressing the issue head-on isn't a fail-safe, although it might be your best option in some cases.

Addressing Setbacks on Your Résumé

What should you say on your résumé? This question clearly makes the list of top ten career anxieties for any worker who has been displaced. Do you show a date range gap? Can you fudge the issue of your termination? Aren't most résumés grossly overstated anyway—so what's a little creative writing going to hurt? Given the amount of creativity that goes into most résumés, it's no wonder we get anxious about the legitimate gaps.

You should start by asking yourself whether there really is an appreciable gap and then addressing what it should say. If you remained on your prior employer's payroll as part of a severance agreement, it's reasonable to say that you need only document the time that started after your last paycheck. A reasonableness test also applies to minor lapses in your past employment record. If you had a one or two-month period during which you were unemployed, I'd simply note the factual dates on your résumé and be done with it. There aren't many managers with that wary an eye. And even if the gap does attract attention, it's really a minor issue.

But what about the case when you had a six-month employment gap? Most likely this period will attract attention. Perhaps during this time you hung out your shingle as an independent consultant. If you made a concerted effort to test your worth as a consultant, list this consulting period on your résumé. If you used the time to volunteer at your local food shelter, put that down as well. I've seen more than one résumé that indicated the person quit their previous job to accomplish a life goal like climbing a mountain or participating in a political campaign—again, worthy of a résumé entry in place of a large gap. If the core reason for your unemployment was because your prior company went belly-up, by all means say so on your résumé. The last line bullet in this section of your experience chronology might read: "Company ceased operations in May, 2004." A prospective employer's biggest fear is hiring a problem employee (someone who was just fired from their previous job), and a résumé gap will often trigger this fear. If there are truthful statements that you can employ that will assuage this fear, so much the better.

What if you were fired from your company? Should you say "terminated on 3/11/03" on your résumé? For an employer, the résumé screening process is one in which he's sorting the wheat from the chafe. Gross inadequacies in skills and experience are cause to toss a résumé, as are indicators of problem employees like large gaps of employment as well as evidence of job hopping. So while I wouldn't advocate lying on your résumé, I also wouldn't advise you to put the word termination on your paper. I'd put the correct dates down, and be prepared to answer the obvious question during the interview. I can tell you from first-hand experience, nothing makes an interview fall flatter than catching someone in a lie. Often someone will come in with a résumé that indicates they are still with their present firm. When it becomes apparent that the person is no longer in the company's employ, it's almost impossible to get past that issue.

What should you say if they ask why you're no longer at the company because you've been fired? Be honest and genuine. If the company was cutting back, and you were one of the most junior people, simply say that. If you and your boss weren't getting along, I'd be sure to assuage any concern that you'll have problems getting along with the next boss. Something like: "While Jack is an awesome leader, there are some personality types that fit better within his system than others. I think I didn't fit his aggressive style." If you were lacking a core skill set, I'd tell them the truth, and the development plan you've embarked on to close this gap.

To Have or Have Not: Employment Contracts

Young people often ask me about employment contracts. Most are in the hopes that they'll prevent a future dire termination if they had one, and they typically want to know when I think they'll have reached a point in their career when they'll be deserving of one of these executive perks. If you're not familiar with the concept, many high-paid executives are under contract with their firms. These contracts are designed to protect the person from negative outcomes, and they typically specify the amount the person will receive if he is fired, how long their benefits will remain in place, etc. A company will often agree to one of these deals as a condition of recruiting a valued executive prospect. The problem often arises when a mid-level person begins a pre-hire negotiation by requesting an employment contract. This demand can raise a red flag with the hiring company, making them wonder why the person wants to spend all his time talking about a negative outcome.

If you're negotiating to be one of the most senior people in the firm then an employment contract might be in the realm of possibility. Outside of that, contain your terms to the offer letter. For example, it's okay to have your offer letter say that you'd receive an extra four weeks of severance pay if the new and speculative division is closed within a year of your arrival. Keeping it reasonable is the key to getting pre-hire protections.

Lesson from Abe Lincoln

Most everyone will experience a firing or layoff at least once in their careers. When that day happens, don't be too hard on yourself for falling short in your job. Abraham Lincoln declared personal bankruptcy, lost his reelection to the U.S. Congress, lost his election for the Senate, and lost his bid for the vice presidency prior to being elected as our sixteenth president. (There doesn't seem to be much argument that he's on the shortlist of our best presidents.) Focus your mental post-mortem on the events that led up to the firing event. If you lost your job because your company wasn't achieving its financial goals, then commit yourself to doing a better job of reading the financial tea leaves the next time, especially if you work for a publicly traded company. There's no excuse for not reading the company's publicly disclosed financial results. If your termination resulted from a lack of skill or experience on your part, then be sure to be more deliberate in your career development process with your next boss. With the formalized process of receiving continuous, constructive feedback from your manager that we discussed in Chapter 5, you'll almost never be the victim of a surprise outcome. For most people, their firing serves as a call to action for their lives. Let's make sure this one is yours as well.

Chapter 15

Going Nowhere Fast

I don't know if I even have an aura, man. I just try to win.

—*Tiger Woods (b. 1975), U.S. golfer*

As people move up through an organization, it's easy to attribute their progress to their superior skills, brain power, or motivation. What is often forgotten is they're *passing* others on their trek to greater responsibility, higher income, and better perks. Someone is winning and someone is losing. In most organizations, there are far more people getting passed over than getting ahead. They come to work every day and they pour their hearts into their work, but others are receiving the promotions, bonuses, and accolades. During internal promotions, it usually works out that there are one or two viable candidates from our employee base. Sure, your company may have a pool of thirty or forty at this level of the organization, but only one or two are obvious choices. So if only one or two have what it takes, what's holding the others back?

In some cases it's as simple an answer as the person doesn't yet have enough experience. That's fine, and time will fix it. Unfortunately, in the majority of cases, it's because of some flaw in the person. It might be the way he presents himself, the way he speaks, or something in his character that's saying *not Bob*. To a manager, it's like shopping for a used car: *This one has lousy paint, this one looks like it's been driven hard, this one is loud and noisy. Ah, this one is in mint condition and is ready for a promotion.* Now, here's the vexing part: most managers don't have the courage or the patience to address these flaws with their people. Sometimes HR rules prevent a manager from engaging an employee in a particular dialogue, and sometimes the employee's ego is just too fragile to hear the feedback. So what happens? Usually the employee hears a line of b.s. from his manager about why Kate got the promotion and how he just needs to "keep at it." Not really knowing the truth, the person wallows with a damaged image, unaware of what he can do to break out of this form of position imprisonment. (I'm using the term *image* to describe the image we create with our behaviors, job performance, actions, and conversations. For the sake of this discussion, I do not mean "image" solely in the physical sense. Although, as we progress with the discussion, you'll see that your physical image does indeed play a significant role in whether you're seen as an "A" player or a "B" player.)

When your manager thinks about you, her opinion transcends the last meeting you had together. She thinks about the whole you, including your dress, attitude, character, speaking style, etc. The sum of all these parts is your image. It's the thing that makes people say, "Jack is a really great guy with a lot to contribute," or "Hank is an old curmudgeon who couldn't manage his way out of a paper bag." When people are off-track in their careers, it's often because their image is negative. People perceive them as possessing one or more undesirable attributes.

In the popular television show *What Not to Wear* the hosts do a makeover on an unsuspecting person. They secretly follow a poorly dressed person through his or her life at home and at work, collecting video clips of mal-dressed moments. They eventually confront the person and lead him or her through a wardrobe makeover that transitions him or her from a slob to a sharp dresser. Wouldn't it be great if we could have the same experience focused on our workplace behavior? Ideally it would happen every few years as a way to tune-up our image. Sure, it would be painful at times, although I suspect the increased income and workplace satisfaction would go a long way towards soothing the minor burn to the ego. One of the challenges we have is that we don't have the ability to see ourselves as we go through life. The view out our eyes is different from the one seen by others. Even the sounds are different. Don't we all hate how we sound on a tape recording? What we think of as being assertive or being a go-getter can be interpreted as obnoxiousness by others. You might think your persona is analytical and introspective, although the bosses in your company might take your silence to mean you're lacking in meaningful contributions to the dialogue.

I've worked with all types of people, with every conceivable image flaw that you can imagine. There was the bright and pretentious Ivy League woman who had the off-putting habit of weaving the name of her school into every conversation. "Well, at Wharton we..." She defined pretentiousness. There was the talented marketing genius who turned into an absolute jerk anytime he had a drink, which turned out to be far too often. We had to keep that one away from client dinners. I worked with an accounting genius who couldn't speak in grown-up grammar. He'd sprinkle "you knows" and "sort ofs" in almost every sentence. Then there was the bright guy who wore bad suits and an even worse toupee. You just couldn't see him as a manager. There were people deemed to be too reticent, too pushy, too arrogant, and untrustworthy, all of whom were out of touch with their self-image.

Now here's the conundrum. The people who really need the help are usually the ones who aren't aware there's a problem. They ask their managers what they need to do to get ahead and rarely will the manager say, "You speak like a valley girl, with all those 'you knows,' 'likes,' and 'totallys'" or, "Your arrogant conversation style is very off-putting to people." Instead, the manager will often make something up, tell a white lie, or shuck and jive around the answer. Instead of the manager addressing an easily correctable problem by saying, "Your speech is very off-putting," the employee continues blissfully along—sideways at primetime in his career. What can you do to make sure this doesn't happen to you? Fortunately, there are some concrete steps you can take to tune-up your image.

Image Evaluation

As any doctor will tell you, you really can't take corrective action without a sound diagnosis. You wouldn't want to start fooling with the formula that defines your identity without knowing what it is that you're trying to fix. I once worked with a woman who was the master of the new look. Every few months she'd come to work with an entirely new physical identity, from her clothes to her hair. This woman had a serious insecurity complex, which reared its ugly head any time she received push back about an opinion or her job performance. She'd verbally snap at her boss or coworkers over the smallest things. I suspect her image makeovers were part and parcel of her making bad guesses about what was wrong with her career. Rather than focus on her workplace behavior, she was off trying to fix something that wasn't broken.

The Early Warning Signs

What should lead you to think you might have a problem in this area? If you're facing one or more of the following career-stalling symptoms, you might be ready for a remediation plan:

1. You've been passed over for one or more promotions within your group. While you're one of the most senior people in the group, others have been getting the choice assignments or promotions.

2. You've been in the same job for a long time and are starting to feel like this might be a career position for you.

3. When the big customer, boss, or partner is coming for a visit, you're never the one picked to participate in the meeting. Whether it involves presenting to the client or a special luncheon, others seem to get the nod.

4. You don't feel like you are fitting in with the organization. Others seem to have strong social ties to each other and enjoy their workplace interactions. You don't seem to have these connections and often feel left out of the mainstream.

5. You've lost one or more jobs when the rationale for your termination wasn't clear. They may have said, "You're not fitting in," or "Your position is being eliminated" when you know it's an important function. Or, you always seem to be on the losing end of the layoff process. (Companies never lay off their best people.)

Getting Help

You suspect there's a problem, now what do you do about it? The first thing you can do is build up your resolve to fix what's broken, no matter how painful it might be. Whenever I take a golf lesson, I can almost be assured that my next few games are going to be erratic as I groove the fix the instructor advocated for me. The same goes for this process. You may be about to hear some very direct and painful feedback. The origins of this issue you're facing might date back to early in your career, perhaps even to your childhood, and facing up to it might cause you considerable angst. Should you do it? Of course you should. Wouldn't you rather go through a few days or weeks of modest emotional turmoil to arrive at a new, better you? It's almost certain you're going to need the help of others to succeed in your transformation. Here are a few places you can go for this help:

1. Arrange your own intervention.

As we discussed in Chapter 5, it's incumbent upon you to position your boss as your personal coach. If you're having a hard time fitting in within your organization or if you're being consistently passed over for promotions, you might want to add your image to the coaching agenda you have with your boss. You might say something like: "Boss, I really value the skills work we've been working on in my development plan. I'm wondering if we could also discuss personality traits as well. If you were to advise me to work on one or two areas of my image, what would they be?" Your manager may be reluctant to bring a sensitive issue up with you on his own, but if you give him an opening like that, he's likely to take it. Now, here's an important point. It's critical that you create an environment of trust when you're having this type of conversation with your boss. If you ask him, "Do you think my appearance is distracting," and then go running to HR when he says you should consider something more conservative, you've blown the trust principle.

2. Consider hiring an image consultant.

An image consultant is a professional who is trained to help people hone rough spots in their public persona. I have recommended them to employees of mine over the years, with remarkable results. A marginally effective sales guy I'll call Harry starting working for me soon after he graduated college. While he brought energy and enthusiasm to the job, in reality he was a quirky and sometimes goofy guy. It always seemed like he'd enter the conversation at the wrong point, and the timing of his humor was even worse. He was poorly dressed and had a strange habit of leaving his mouth open as he worked. How this guy made it through our college hiring program, I'll never know. But, somehow he ended up being my problem. I gained a certain respect for how hard he was willing to work, so rather than cutting him loose, we embarked on a fix-it plan.

In one of our coaching sessions, I brought up the idea of him seeing an image consultant. I told him that I didn't think he had a good handle on his self-image and that it might be good to get some help from an expert. We discussed the short- and long-term benefits, and he reluctantly agreed. The results? Astounding. His image consultant spent a great deal of time gathering data on him. She spoke with a few of his friends, as well as a few of us at the office. She videotaped him in a number of simulations, including when he made customer calls, a presentation, and even when he walked to and from his car. Along the way, she pointed out problems with his dress, posture, and open mouth. She taught him techniques for gracefully entering into a conversation, and bowing out. Her lunches with him led to a few etiquette tips, including correcting his strange tendency to hold his fork like a child. She convinced him that good joke timing is a genetically determined attribute, and he didn't have the gene. She fixed a weak handshake, a perennially crooked tie, and a failure to look people in the eye. In a few short weeks, she fixed years worth of flaws. The makeover was truly remarkable to everyone who knew him in the before context. Today he's an outstanding sales professional who would make any employer proud.

3. Hire a fashion consultant.

Before you laugh, let me say that this is something I think everyone should do at least once in their professional life. Really. In the introduction of this book I promised there would be no bullshit, so here's a truth that you need to know: physical appearance matters in the business world. Countless studies have proven that physical attractiveness contributes to career success. I wouldn't advocate spending much time on pulling a Michael Jackson, although I think it would be well worth your time to invest in your wardrobe, hair, and hygiene.

While the TV airways are filled with radical makeovers, there's a real world where experts help people tune-up their physical image. What can a fashion consultant do for you? She can essentially give you a palate in which you can work. They're expert at defining appropriate color ranges for various skin and hairs colors. They can tell you what silhouettes (the way clothes drape) work with your body type and give you buying advice for building a lasting wardrobe. Let's face it. Most of us see a different person in the mirror than what others truly see. Many of these experts will go shopping with you for a relatively small cost. In the end, you'll save money, as you'll be buying fewer higher quality things, and you'll feel and look more confident.

4. **Work through difficult emotional issues with a qualified professional.**

It may be that the issue you're facing is of the deep-rooted emotional variety. Perhaps it's a long-held insecurity that makes you so aggressive or your tendency to need lots of support (your boss would say you're needy) relates to a parent who was always putting you down. Spending time with a qualified therapist could help you in ways that you can't imagine. Trust me, more than a few of my former employees could have benefited from a few conversations with a qualified professional. One new innovation in this area is the life coach. Life coaches are people who are trained to help others work through issues, and it's all done over the phone. If you search for one on the Internet, you may be surprised to see they exist in great numbers, and in many flavors. Some specialize in certain professions and others on particular issues (like obsessiveness).

Stay and Fix or Leave and Restart

A difficult issue you may face is whether it's actually possible to overcome an image flaw at your present company. If you ultimately learn that the problem with your career has been that your assertive personality has been perceived as abusive to your coworkers, it might take several years after you've fixed the problem to convince them that you're really a nice guy. The question becomes whether you'd be better off leaving and implementing the new you at a different company. Here are a few thoughts to guide your thinking:

1. It's a good idea to diagnose and implement the fix at your present company. Your present job and company is familiar to you, and there's no sense in changing too many variables at the same time. Additionally, a new employer might do some informal reference checking on you, so you'd rather have them saying, "He used to have problems with being aggressive with the administrative staff, although lately I'd say he's been improving in that area.

2. If the thing that has been holding you back involves emotional scars and bruises at your present company, I'd advise seeking new employment once you're well on the road to fixing the problem. Bruises of this sort tend to last a long time—probably longer than you'll want to invest. If you've been know as "Brenda the witch" for the past few years, you're probably better off becoming "Brenda the star" at another locale.

3. If the issue you are facing is more tactical, for example you dress poorly, I'd plan to stick around at your present company. Not only will it be noticed that you've changed, they'll also soon forget what you looked like in your previous image.

4. If you work in a small industry, where everyone knows each other, you may be better served sticking it out and

implementing the "new you" at your present employer. Chances are your reputation is preceding you, and short of an industry change, you're going to need to convince those around you that you've made big improvements.

Your Picture-Perfect Career

Brainpower can be an overused measure in the corporate arena. Sure, there are lots of people with 140 IQs that do well in the workplace. There are also many people with a more average 120 score that go on to be titans of industry. The obsession we have about "smart people" is misplaced. Yes, an organization needs big thinkers, but it also needs sharp, crisp people who can implement ideas that come from the brainiacs. For the vast majority of under-performers who have worked for me, IQ enhancement wouldn't be at the top of my three wishes list for them. I'd sooner see them get a dose of common sense, better customer presentability, improved speaking skills, or a sprinkle of charm that will improve their relations with their coworkers. It's not their brains that are not working; it's their image. Top performers have the total package—from image to competence.

Chapter 16

"Help! I Hate My Job!"

Turn the clock to zero, boss
The river's wide, we'll swim across
Started up a brand new day

—*Sting (b. 1951), British musician, "Brand New Day"*

If you've come to the conclusion that your job or profession isn't for you, you're in plentiful company. The book *What Color is Your Parachute?*, the consummate find-a-new-profession book, has sold over eight million copies in the past few decades. Each copy was presumably purchased by someone who came to the conclusion that life's too short to spend it doing this lousy job. In 1968 Lyndon Johnson announced to the nation that he was quitting his job as our thirty-sixth president. He was living in a pressure cooker and decided it wasn't worth it. Each and every day, executives walk away from corner offices, athletes decide they've had enough, and politicians decide they don't want to run again. Maybe there's something inside you saying *time to go.*

This chapter is designed to guide your thinking as you contemplate a major career move. Rather than focusing on helping you choose a new vocation, which could be an entire book in itself, it's about helping you get yourself in the right decision making mindset.

Reality Check

Coming to grips with your dislike for your job or profession is an emotionally draining experience. It might start with a feeling of malaise or mild depression as you begin to lose desire for your field of work. It often leads to diminished work performance and a new element of workplace stress: the boss riding you for performance issues. If you're not loving your job, it's hard to love the work. As you come to grips with your need to do something else, you add a new layer of stress to your life. You now have to figure out what career would be best for you, plan a job search, and face a potential reduction in income as you become a newbie again in another field or company. As you move closer to making the decision to take action, you layer on yet another level of stress: you've got to tell people close to you what's going on. These people might be parents who paid for the education that got you into the now-hated career, your friends who will think you've got an attention deficit disorder, a spouse who will now have to carry a larger part of the financial load, or a boss who has invested time in mentoring you. If it sounds like a stress hairball, it is. A major career course correction may be one of the most stressful things you do in life.

Where should you start on this introspective journey? Start with the reality that you're about to burn some very expensive bullets. A professional has a scarce number of change bullets they can fire in a given career. You've got four or five company change bullets, let's call them silver bullets, and one gold one you can use on a major change in professions. In other words, you can change jobs or professions, but you can't do it often. You've got only so much time in the formative years of your career to establish a trajectory towards your goals. If you spend most of this time jumping from one career strategy to the next, you'll burn too much time at the bottom of the corresponding pyramids. Think of it this way: what does it look like to a company when a thirty-something person walks in with a résumé full of unrelated job experiences? The term *job hopper* comes to mind. Companies are much more inclined to be attracted to a candidate who knows where he's going, with a résumé that illustrates a great deal of continuity in his career progression. This shouldn't be interpreted to mean that you can't change jobs or professions. You can—but not often. A major career change should be looked at as a serious endeavor requiring a substantial amount of thought. You want to get this next one right.

If you're contemplating a change in professions, this retrenching process necessitates a substantial rework of your life skills pyramid. In some cases it's going to mean throwing away some of your hard-earned experiences, and in others it might cause retrenching back to the beginning. I have a friend who was a marketing executive who decided that his real passion in life was wine. He made this discovery in his forties and decided that he wanted to spend the last twenty years of his career doing something more enjoyable. His new pyramid blocks? The first one was as a sales clerk in a gourmet wine store. It was the only way he could find to break into this industry. From the corner office to wearing a clerk's apron. And his corresponding salary cut was, well, breathtaking. Now, he'll tell you he's never been happier—and it's true—but he's also cognizant of the immense financial cost and risks he undertook to make this life-altering decision.

Real or an Illusion?

Before deciding that you've got to make a career change, let's first decide whether a move is truly warranted. Ask yourself these questions:

1. What's the view from your pyramid?

When you took this job you thought it was going to provide you with certain skills and experiences. Maybe the boss is a jerk, or you're just not interested in the paper business, but the stress-reducing question is whether your pyramid is getting what it needs from this job. If this job is giving you what you signed up for, you might be better off plodding along, with an eye on making the major change downstream. Often in these situations you need to put your emotions aside for the greater good of your pyramid.

2. Do you hate your job or love an illusion?

There's a tendency for people to think there's a better, more lucrative, and less stressful job waiting in another industry. They walk around with this notion that *their* industry is the pressure cooker and that others are having much more fun in their jobs. This illusion is often fed by their friends. At its most basic core, a human is programmed to create envy in others. Do you think the person who drives the BMW is really doing it for the rack and pinion steering? Hardly. He's doing it to make other people envious of him. Keeping up with the Joneses is really about the Joneses making others *want* to keep up with them. When someone talks about how great their job is, or how much money they are making, it's easy for you to conclude that your job or profession is somehow inferior. In reality, I bet I could shoot you and your friend up with truth serum and extract confessions that you've got similar ups, downs, fears, stresses, and frustrations. If all jobs were easy, they'd pay minimum wage. And, if you're running from a profession because of the stress or frustrations, you'll likely find similar frustrations in your next job.

We all experience a voyeuristic type of infatuation with jobs that we view at from afar. This type of attraction isn't too different from the kind we feel for strangers at a distance. It's not until we meet them up close do we realize they talk funny or they're insensitive or arrogant. I was always infatuated with the idea of being an airline pilot. Flying that big machine to far-off places, while working seven days a month with free travel perks, seemed like the ultimate job. That is, until I became a private pilot and met a bunch of airline pilots. I learned that for the first half of your career the pay is low, the far-off places reserved for low seniority pilots are usually small backwater towns served by commuter aircraft, and the free airline tickets aren't much of a value if you can't afford hotels. In the second half of your career you're likely to face a bankruptcy or two; and if you're forced to change airlines, you start back at the beginning of the seniority list (back to low pay and lousy destinations). The grass is almost always greener in the other industry.

Time for a Change—Now What?

Let's say that after careful thought and consideration you've concluded that you really need a change. What do you do now? March in and tell your boss that you're quitting? Not so fast; there's still work to be done. Before doing anything, you really need to do some homework that will ensure you expend this silver bullet wisely. Essentially, you need to get to the bottom of your unhappiness so you don't put yourself back in the same situation (with one less silver bullet). Over the years, I have seen people do numerous versions of this jumping from the frying pan into the fire. More than once, I have spent time with a person coming to grips with the reality that her job might not be for her. Sometimes it's a poor skills fit, and other times it has to do with the stresses of the job. So what happens next? She takes a similar job with a different company. The person goes on to find herself in the same failure cycle, this time with less time remaining in the game, a choppier résumé, and once less silver bullet. Here are some guidelines you need to consider before you make your next move.

What Makes You Unhappy?

While it might seem paradoxical to start with what makes you unhappy, we need to go there before writing a prescription for making you happier in your career. By understanding how your present job is falling short, we can better calibrate a plan for the future. Try to answer the following questions as honestly as you can:

1. Is it your job or external factors?

It's important to determine whether the source of your unhappiness is being driven by outside influences. Maybe it's a problematic relationship with a boss or coworker, or maybe it's your hour-and-fifteen-minute commute. Write a list entitled "The ten things I hate about this job." What do you come up with?

2. Is it your work performance?

No one feels great about their job when their performance is lacking. Often the first instinct is to make a change— before the company changes you. There's a chance you're miscast for your job and an equally high chance that you're being put into a tough position. If you're a stockbroker during a market meltdown, you shouldn't be too hard on yourself. Similarly, if you're an engineer on a high-pressure project that's woefully behind schedule due to a disorganized project manager, that's hardly cause for jumping ship. This project too shall end. In most cases, if you have a specific performance deficiency, you'd be better served staying in the job and working collaboratively with your boss on an improvement plan. Bolting because you're lacking certain skills is like playing whack-a-mole; most likely you'll see that performance issue again at your next job.

3. Is it the company or the industry?

If you're working for a poorly managed company in a high-growth industry, it might be as simple as moving upstream to a better firm. If, on the other hand, you work in the newspaper industry that has seen its daily circulation and employment numbers falling precipitously following the advent of the Internet, then an industry change might be a good direction. There's a tendency for people to be too focused on the headlines about their company. A desire to be playing for the winning team often makes people want to change companies. Make sure you project your loyalties at your pyramid rather than a company logo. Each block of your pyramid is designed to provide you with certain skills and experiences. If your mid-sized company is giving you a rich environment to build out one or more pyramid blocks, there's no need to think wistfully about working for World Domination, Inc.

4. Is it about money?

Anytime you find yourself contemplating a major career move over money, you should force yourself into a disciplined thought process. Sure, we all work for money, and the more of it the better, but money is just one component of a happy career. Whenever someone waves more money in front of me I apply a simple formula. Divide the amount of the raise by two (because governments always seem to find a way to take half of my paycheck), and then divide the result by twenty-four, which is the number of paychecks I get in a year. If someone offers you another $30K per year to change jobs, we're really talking about $625 per paycheck ([$30,000 ÷ 2] x 24 = $625). If the output of this formula isn't a life-changing amount of money, you owe it to yourself to weigh it heavily against the goals articulated in your pyramid. The goal of your pyramid is to maximize a five to ten million dollar income stream—not to opportunistically seize $625 raises.

I have many friends who are lawyers, and I divide them into two camps: those who went into law for the money and those who did it for the love of participating in the legal process. Those who did it for the money all seem to be casting about for a new career in their late forties. They learned that law can be a complex and monotonous world that happens to pay well. The same goes for the other sure-fire 1980s career choice: medicine. The doctor who made the for-the-money choice back in the 80s is now a disillusioned soul as he fights to keep his head up in the new world of managed care insurance. He's probably also the guy his patients gripe about for not having a good bedside manner. Doing it for the love of medicine would have made for a much happier existence.

5. Is your unhappiness temporary or permanent?

We all have our ups and down, as our companies do. Just when we think we can't stand another day with our lousy boss, he gets fired and replaced by an awesome leader. If there's one place you don't want to be rash, it's in the matter of your career. A major career move should be a thoughtful process that involves introspection and contemplation.

6. Are you still learning?

The ultimate gauge of whether it's time to change is whether you're still learning in your present job. Your skills pyramid is essentially a learning pyramid where you gather key experiences that position you for the next opportunity. If your boss sucks, or you have fallen out of love with your industry but you're still learning, it might be wise to stay. You need to look at every job as a unique opportunity to acquire certain skills, and if you leave before you have everything you can get out of this job, you might not get an opportunity to go back and repeat this pyramid block. You'll also find this to be a great coping strategy. If you're constantly taking stock of a job based on what you're learning as opposed to what you're achieving, it's likely you'll experience less workplace stress.

Taking Action

If after answering these questions you are still convinced that you need to make a move, then putting an action plan together becomes the next priority. It's a deliberate process that's going to take time. A really great career is a forty-year building process and anytime you find yourself thinking about a quick fix, you should stop yourself from acting on this fallacy. One of the advantages of the pyramid method of career planning is that you've carved your profession into manageable chapters versus looking at as one long narrative. Being able to say "this chapter will end before too long" will serve to reduce your stress because you're not looking at the situation as an intractable problem. When your mind drifts to your dissatisfaction with your present job, focus your mind on what you're learning versus what you're doing.

You first need to decide whether you need to make a tactical or strategic move. A tactical move would be best defined as making an adjustment. The most basic of tactical moves might involve you changing departments or going to work on a different team with a better boss. A more serious tactical move might involve a job or company change within the same industry. In essence, you're keeping the same profession with an adjustment to your plan of attack. By definition, your skills pyramid will involve many tactical moves, all aligned towards helping you achieve your goals.

A strategic move is a whole different animal. It usually involves shooting a gold bullet, meaning a change of professions is in the offing. Try to make these moves as early as possible in your career. You probably remember the high school math lessons on compounding in which you learned that the dollars you sock away in your twenties are worth nearly ten times more than the dollars you save in your fifties. The same goes for your career ($10,000 invested at 8 percent at age twenty-five will be worth $217,000 when you're sixty-five. The same $10K invested at age fifty-five will be worth $20K). Your salary is subject to the same compounding formula if you don't have major disruptions to the salary increase process. Each year when you get a raise, the percentage increase is based on the prior year's salary. Let's say that you start in the workforce earning $40,000 per year and receive raises averaging 8 percent per year (including annual raises and promotions). If you compound these raises, meaning you add a raise each year, you'll be making $80,000 after ten years, $170,000 after twenty years, and if you retire in your fortieth year you'll be making $800,000 annually. If these numbers sound large, remember inflation averages 4 percent per year. In this scenario, your lifetime earnings are $10.3 million. Now, what's the picture look like if you make a major career change in your tenth year, necessitating a 40 percent pay cut as part of the restart? Would you believe your new lifetime earnings will be $6.4 million? That's a $4 million reduction in your lifetime earnings due to the concept of compounding. I'd be wrong not to mention that people some-times switch professions to exit a low-paying industry to enter a higher-paying one. While this is true, much larger populations of people seem to cast about between equally paying industries, although they take pay cuts each time they cross profession boundaries.

Loading the Gold Bullet

You hate your profession, and you need to put that gold bullet in the chamber. What next? The obvious place to start is your pyramid. While you've always wanted to be a sports agent, it might be nearly impossible to get there from your present position as a twenty-eight-year-old customer service assistant. You might be better served by identifying those professions that both interest you as well as salvage some of the blocks of your present pyramid. Let's say you came out of school as an electrical engineer and have a pyramid that says chief engineering officer in its top block. If you've found engineering too tedious and can't see yourself in a technical role sitting behind a computer for the next forty years, perhaps instead of considering going back to school to study law you should consider a career in technical sales or consulting. These roles will allow you to exercise your business and people skills and largely leverage the technical foundation you've created in the first row of your pyramid.

Keep in mind that as you plot your strategy you need to be thinking at least two moves ahead. You wouldn't want to focus on a particular job that corresponds with your career change plans without also knowing the job you're going to focus on next, as well as your Plan B strategy. Between these two objectives, I'd put a slightly higher priority on having your Plan B scenarios well thought out. While a mid-career profession change is stressful, a misfire in your new profession offers the potential of devastating consequences. Failing to successfully latch on in your first job within your new profession would look bad on paper as well as leaving you far fewer options of where to go next. Think positive, but plan negatively.

I have a friend who I'll call Tom who was a well-known corporate lawyer. His specialty was corporate transaction work, where he represented corporations in mergers, acquisitions, and financings. While he was great at his job, something was missing. He grew tired of "turning pages" on large documents and started to find that there was little differentiation between one deal and the next. He had already made partner with his firm so there really weren't any titles left for him to earn. Much of his job involved him dealing with entrepreneurs, and he came to the conclusion that he would be better cast as an entrepreneur. Now let's think about this for a minute. Here was a guy making serious money as a very competent lawyer who just decided to cash it all in for one of the most risky choices he could make. The very best entrepreneurs have a 50:50 hit rate. A new one? Try one in ten odds. You can probably already guess what happened; Tom crashed and burned. This was one of the more catastrophic career failures I have witnessed. The large client base he had built up over the years had selected new attorneys. Going back to law would have meant starting over again, so he was basically back to the beginning, at age thirty-five.

What could Tom have done differently? Risk mitigation would have been a good place to start. Perhaps there was another career field that would have allowed him to scratch his need-for-change itch, without going to the far end of the risk/reward continuum. What was missing in his career. The chance to advance? Relationships with others? Travel? If he had developed a "what makes me unhappy" list he might have a lower risk solution to his problem. A competent career counselor might have helped him work through his choices. He had selected a high-tech field which was entirely new to him. Maybe he would have been better off joining an existing high-tech company focused on making software for the legal industry. This action would have allowed him to ease his way into high-tech and reduce the chance that he'd flame out in his first job in a new profession. The moral of the story: when you're shooting the gold bullet, you really want to make sure you're aiming in the right place.

The funk that corresponds with job stress serves as a cautionary tale. When we pour everything we have into our jobs, we enter the danger zone that our jobs become the way we define ourselves. When things at work are great, life is great. And…when work stinks, life stinks. If you work fifty hours per week, which ends up occupying about 30 percent of your time, make sure there are plenty of other diversions in the other 70 percent of your life.

The actions you take in response to your realization that you don't like your job have serious implications. If you handle this well, you can position yourself on a happier and more rewarding path. Done poorly, you could significantly harm your lifetime earnings and potentially leave yourself stranded between two worlds. Unless the situation is absolutely dire, remember to take things slow. Give yourself time for thought and introspection, and make your move when you have the most certainty that your move will succeed.

In the end, career happiness is a worthy objective. I hope you haven't gotten the wrong message in this chapter. If you hate your job and the situation isn't fixable, then you should absolutely make a change. Life's too precious to spend it doing something that makes you unhappy. The key is to make your change a deliberate and thoughtful process, aimed at delivering you to a better place. If I had one wish for the readers of this book it would be that they find happiness in their careers. Career happiness isn't something that happens but rather something you do. I wish you all the best in this worthwhile journey.

Author's Note

I hope you've come to see your career as a journey. A forty-year trek to accomplish your goals and aspirations. As an author, my goals have been modest. I'll have accomplished my objective if I got you thinking about the critical success factors for your career. My greatest hope is that I'll somehow make your journey more rewarding, fun, or less stressful. A friend of mine says life's too short to drink bad wine. I feel the same way about our careers. Life's too short to spend it not achieving your potential.

If you've been wondering during your reading what's with all the aviation metaphors in this book, I'll tell you now that I'm a pilot. The format I've chosen mimics that of the pilot operating manual of an airplane—the how-to book that teaches us how to fly the machine. Typically the first three-quarters of the manual is labeled "normal procedures," and the remaining portion is called "emergency procedures." This "red" section covers things like a stuck landing gear, an engine problem, or an instrumentation failure. The last few chapters of this book will serve to guide you through career emergencies, ranging from hating your job to getting laid off or fired. You can read them now, or refer to them later.

Where can you go from here? I have assembled some additional resources for you on the Internet. If you point your browser at www.mkt10.com you'll find a set of tools that will help you get more from the book. Among them you'll find a pyramid builder that might help you with your career plan. If you're curious about the Mkt10.com URL, it's the home of my newest entrepreneurial endeavor. After selling the CareerBuilder Corporation, I took some time off to spend more time with my family and to write this book. In 2004, feeling reenergized, I set out to build another company. Mkt10 is an entirely new online job marketplace, designed to give top performers a new place to find great jobs. I thoroughly enjoyed building CareerBuilder, although every entrepreneur has the dream of one day being able to start over with a clean sheet of paper. At this writing, I had called up the old members of the band with the mission of creating the next generation in online career sites.

One the most exciting aspects of Mkt10 is the feedback it provides to the job seeker. It will tell you which jobs are the best match for your experience and skills, it will tell you whether a company is interested in you, and what adjustments you need to make on your "want list" to improve your chances of getting hired. Jobseekers used to complain to me about "the black hole effect" of submitting a résumé and never hearing anything from the company. One of the design goals of Mkt10 is to make sure everyone knows where they stand, at all times. The early feedback has been very positive. Feel free to visit the site at www.mkt10.com.

If you liked this book, or have suggestions for improvement, I'd love to hear from you. You can reach me at RMcGovern@mkt10.com. I promise to personally respond to each and every email. If we don't talk, I wish you 10,000 days of career happiness.

Index